GEORGE C. HILL

It's Way Out in the West!

Pembrokeshire: From prehistory to online dating (with some mermaids, ghosts and conspiracy thrown in)

Copyright © 2021 by George C. Hill

All rights reserved. No part of this publication may be reproduced, stored or transmitted in any form or by any means, electronic, mechanical, photocopying, recording, scanning, or otherwise without written permission from the publisher. It is illegal to copy this book, post it to a website, or distribute it by any other means without permission.

George C. Hill asserts the moral right to be identified as the author of this work.

George C. Hill has no responsibility for the persistence or accuracy of URLs for external or third-party Internet Websites referred to in this publication and does not guarantee that any content on such Websites is, or will remain, accurate or appropriate.

Designations used by companies to distinguish their products are often claimed as trademarks. All brand names and product names used in this book and on its cover are trade names, service marks, trademarks and registered trademarks of their respective owners. The publishers and the book are not associated with any product or vendor mentioned in this book.

None of the companies referenced within the book have endorsed the book.

First edition

A sideways glance at the county of Pembrokeshire. From its natural past to the present age, where ancient magic meets the modern.

George C. Hill

1 WHO ARE THE PEMBROKESHIRE PEOPLE? WHY WE ARE WELSH BUT NOT WELSH?   1

2 PEMBROKESHIRE IN WINTER VS IN SUMMER: WEIRD WEATHER, TORNADOES AND LONE LIGHTNING CLOUDS   9

3 WHO RUNS PEMBROKESHIRE?!   15

4 PEMBROKESHIRE JUST DOESN'T SELL IT: THE HIDDEN IN PLAIN SIGHT LINKS TO A FAMOUS PAST   21

5 A NATURAL EDGE, BEAUTIFUL LANDSCAPE, DRUNK WORKMEN AND THE LOST STONE ARCH OF SAUNDERSFOOT   29

6 GHOSTS   34

7 NORTH PEMBROKESHIRE   42

8 PICKING UP IN PEMBROKESHIRE - A GUIDE TO STEPPING OUT   46

9 ONLINE DATING IN PEMBROKESHIRE   52

10 WHERE DID ALL THE COCAINE COME FROM?   56

11 THE 'LOST WORLDS': LICENSED PREMISES THAT ARE LEGEND IN PEMBROKESHIRE (MY SELECFION)   60

12 MORE STAR WARS CONNECTIONS, NUCLEAR WASTE STORAGE, UFO'S AND TOP-SECRET DRONE TESTING   67

13 MAGIC ANCIENT PLACES, BLACK PANTHERS AND ELVIS PRESELI   73

14 THE MERMAID OF FRESHWATER EAST   79

15 PEMBROKESHIRE AND THE OTHERWORLD: WITCHES, WIZARDS, AND MAGIC   90

16 PEMBROKESHIRE FOREVER -- LET US DRIFT WITH THE TIDES   102

Acknowledgement

Thanks to the world for being so strange in the relatively early 21st century as to have sent me back west with nothing to do but this.

Thanks to my family and friends -- to Mum, Dad, Chris, Damien, Mr Griffith, Peter, Hugh, Ben, Amir, Gavin, Leon, Alan, Ian, Oliver, Jerry, Tiggy, Kazzy, Tom, Will, Sarah as well as others, for everything.

This book is for Becky.

1

Who are the Pembrokeshire People? Why we are Welsh but not Welsh?

Little England beyond Wales

This is a book for those of you needing an insight into the cosmic people that inhabit the land of Pembrokeshire as well as the nature of the place itself. The historical and contemporary strangeness, darkness and beauty, even some of the banality of Pembrokeshire will be contained herein! There will be many a truth that needed telling within this work and many a character a local person may recognise. The town of Tenby, given its importance to the economy and fame of 'south' Pembrokeshire especially, will be important to these pages. I do not intend on insulting anyone in particular - but the truth will out. That said, this book is written by a South Pembrokeshire boy and therefore will also contain a thoroughly healthy dollop of probable nonsense.

There is no traditional 'ark' or any particularly linear progression within these pages. No, instead treat this tome as a locally themed pack of cards and read them as they are dealt. I will be your local croupier.

I grew up in the village of Penally. Penally is a village in the south of the county of Pembrokeshire. It is situated on the coast and next to the better- known town of Tenby. Pembrokeshire (at least South Pembrokeshire) is quite different from almost all other counties in Wales in that it feels more like being in Britain than in the small principality of Wales that helps form the union of the UK. The coastal parts of the county rely heavily on tourism and though a sizeable portion of the seasonal visitors are from the run down and barbarous valleys of South Wales, so there are considerable numbers that come on holiday hailing from cities across the UK. Many of these visitors, over the decades, would enjoy their holidays so much that they would eventually come and live in Pembrokeshire. Villages near the sea in Pembrokeshire are made up in large part of retirees, even middle-aged couples that have accents that originated in a quite different region. The indigenous locals, however, have a Pembrokeshire accent that is subtle and innocuous but also distinct in that it is easy enough on the ear. The Pembrokeshire accent sounds rather like the rural coastal accents found in Norfolk or around Cornwall - seasoned with Richard Burton and possibly a pinch of Ruth Madoc just for musicality. It has a Welsh lilt only, not the almost bawdy tone that emanates to the east of the Landsker line as Pembrokeshire ends and the wilds of Carmarthenshire and beyond hove into view. The 'Landsker line' is, in all intents and purposes, a border between South and North Pembrokeshire and the eastern part of Pembrokeshire with Carmarthenshire. Some people call it an 'imaginary' line but in fact it is, or certainly was, a militarised delineation made of fortresses, the ruins of which for the most part are still standing. The fortresses and castles were built by the Norman invaders to essentially keep the Welsh at bay and to limit their chance of disturbing the important south Pembrokeshire towns and ports. The Welsh that remained in the southern part of this border would be different culturally to all other Welsh and I hope to explain more about that as we go.

The people of south Pembrokeshire at least, are more open minded to people 'from away' than their cousins across other parts of Wales. The sense of 'Welshness' in Pembrokeshire is more patriotic than nationalistic (except maybe on rugby international 'match days'). You do not often see Welsh flags flying like in many other regions of Wales and even those that are born and bred in Pembrokeshire will often have English blood on one side of their immediate family. The history of why this is the case is certainly in part due to the tourism factor already mentioned, but also, and more crucially regarding the point of the county's 'Britishness' - a history from 1000 years prior is needed to be understood. I'll certainly attempt, just for you, to note down some of the essential elements and events that have conspired to create 'little England beyond Wales' and its people. Do not, some of you more Welsh precious types, start to panic. I will not attempt an anglicisation of Pembrokeshire, but the reality of the south of the county at least is more red, white and blue in feeling than Celtic dragon. A British Welsh rather than a Welsh British milieu has been established over the past millennium or so.

Remarkably, given the interesting and fairly unique nature of the sociologi- cal history of Pembrokeshire (this also goes for the geological history) is that the people of the county, in the main, are quite ignorant of their collective background. The truth of the matter is that the county of Pembrokeshire and especially south Pembrokeshire has much of its history directly forged by invaders with sentiments without an iota of welsh feeling. The once strategically important town of Pembroke was in pre-Norman times a trading port and crossing point to Ireland. The town was important for connection to the Viking stronghold of the city of Dublin, for the Scandinavian element, known as, appropriately enough, the Vikings. Many of the places, towns, and villages in the county, have Nordic (and some Saxon) echoes.

The Scandinavian invaders of the first millennium certainly left their mark. Ancient Viking sounds forming words such as Freystrop (a derivation of Freya's Thorpe. Freya is the Norse Goddess of Love and Thorpe is a village or hamlet), Caldey, and Skomer are familiar descriptors. One village, Bubbaston, is possibly named after the Viking Warlord Ubba whose fleet was moored after a storm at nearby Milford Haven just long enough for the Viking men to frequent and form 'relations' with many of the (one must assume) captivated 9th century Welsh ladies. The juxtaposition between the almost swarthy native Welsh men, barrel chested, stocky with brown eyes and dark hair and the chiselled, sea faring, tall blond-blue eyed warriors from another world must have caused many a double take. An awful lot of coitus between the Nordic visitors and Welsh ladies ensued over the months it took the Viking sailors to rebuild their ships. No prizes for guessing that a job that should have taken weeks somehow or other ended up taking months! It has been said in other literature on the area that Ubba and his men did in fact change the DNA of Pembrokeshire forever. There is certainly a less homogenised look to the South Pembs people than when you travel further into Wales. This may well be in part because of Ubba and his fleet's visit to Milford Haven in the late 800's. Ubba and his men's escapades with local Pembrokeshire ladies is, in contemporary times, saluted in its own way by the British Army 'squaddies' that frequent the pubs and nightclubs of the county when stationed in the many military bases in the area.

Later in the history of Pembrokeshire and after the Viking hordes raped and pillaged the land came the Norman dynasties. Actually, it is incorrect to say the Normans were an entirely different people to the Vikings... the Normans, in actual fact, were in origin Viking invaders that set up the Dukedom of Normandy in the 10th and 11th centuries, but I digress.

The Norman elites that took over England and Wales after the 1066 invasion by William the 1st (also known as William 'the Bastard' for familial reasons as well as the reason you might assume one would pick up such an epithet) would covet Pembrokeshire for its woodland and fishing. The strategically important town of Pembroke would get a castle and defensive towers very soon after William's initial invasion. The town's links to Viking Dublin were still especially important in the 11th century. Norman elites would have had a knowledge of the area passed down from Viking to Norman families that far predated the Norman conquest of England. Pembrokeshire would be of such importance to William's fourth child Henry (the 1st of England) that when hints of Welsh insurrection in the area now known as South Pembrokeshire at the turn of the 12th century were heard in the royal court, Henry took drastic action that would shape the cultural anomalies seen in the county today... Ever wondered why the south Pembrokeshire accent is different and far less pronounced than accents in all other parts of Wales? Ever wondered why there are ancient Flemish chimneys dotted about the landscape? Well, if you have not then you probably should have thought about it. After all, we are as far West of England as you can be in Wales (and an awfully long way from Holland and Belgium) and are much closer to Ireland – a fact that could help explain the Pembrokeshire person's almost puritanical belief in and love of, the humble potato. Well, the reason for the subtle accent and the strange low country architectural influence is down to king Henry in and around 1100. Basically, Henry got irritated by the pre-Norman invasion influential Welsh contingent that were intent on the quite impossible retaking of estates and land etc. Welsh uprising of any kind was stopped in its tracks by Henry when he instructed that hundreds of suspected rebels face the choice of exile to the wild and mysterious north of the county and past the Landsker line -- or death. The Welsh rebel element in the south of the county were soon either dead or living in North Pembrokeshire. A choice I'm glad I never had to make. Also, just to alter the Welsh influence in the important region of south Pembrokeshire still further, Henry would extend invitations to many Flemish peoples living in England to come set up home in the area. So, with one stroke Henry solved two problems. He sent the Flemings to Pembrokeshire with promises of land there. But more importantly they could help to keep order. In fact, there were well over 2000 new Flemish settlers in the area within a year or two, an extraordinary amount to add quickly to the medieval area of what now roughly comprises South Pembrokeshire (the area then known as Ross). These former residents of the low countries, but also England, spoke a dialect of Flemish similar to what was heard and understood in non-Celtic parts of Britain. Not only did these new settlers erect strange chimneys that were built to last, but their Flemish English/Saxon language become established in the region of Ross in 'Dyvet' or as you know it – Dyfed. This literal history lesson is almost over don't worry. But let us just quickly pick up on what a contemporary commentator said of these events at their time of undertaking. Caradoc of Llancarfan explains it better than me:

> *In the year 1108 the rage of the sea did overflow and drowne a great part of the lowe countrie of Flanders in such sort that the inhabitants were driven to seek themselves other dwelling places, who came to King Henrie and desired him to give them some void place to remain in, who being verie liberall of that which was not his owne, gave them the land of Ros in Dyvet or West Wales, where Pembroke, Tenby and Haverford are now built, and where they remaine to this daie, as may well be perceived by their speach and condition farre differing from the rest of the countrie.*

These same Fleming would also bring to Pembrokeshire their Corgi dog breed which they used for herding farm animals. This breed now known as Pembrokeshire Corgis would famously become the favourite of Queen Elizabeth II. Welsh villages often have the uniquely welsh ecclesiastic prefix 'Llan', but thanks to the events explained above so Pembrokeshire is full of another prefix of English origin, namely, St. (St Florence, St Ishmaels, St Brides, St Dogmaels etc). The suffix 'ston' is also common and ends many English or old English sounding names for many villages and hamlets in Pembrokeshire (Bosherston, Hodgeston, Wiston, Gumfreston and many more). I suppose to us in Pembrokeshire and particularly to those in south Pembs, none of this is peculiar, but to people from other Welsh counties these anglicised elements helping to form the nomenclature of the area are more noticeable. I remember as a child finding a 'proper' Welsh accent rather grating and many times I have heard friends 'taking the piss' with over-the-top take offs of a 'real' Welsh accent (usually with a Swansea lilt) asking, 'alrite butt'!? 'Ow's it g'wann'!? And fackin' ell' etc. Is it possible even, that the 'real' Welsh people could foster some suspicion of Pembrokeshire folk regarding the county's differences? I would say in many cases this is entirely likely.

Most of the trouble in Tenby in the summer months will often be from 'valley commandos' (people from the south Welsh valleys) fighting with local drinkers as well as pub and club security (doormen). There have been many cases, well documented, where police numbers in Tenby in particular, in the summer months, are not at a level to be commensurate to the threat posed by street crime in the town, especially when the population can increase 10-fold from July to September. Add to this a new local drug problem thanks to Tenby's links to organised criminal routes and networks involving cocaine; and there is much to ponder regarding the preservation of peace in the busy summer months in Pembrokeshire (Please see chapter 10 for more on this). The homogeny and population of Pembrokeshire and in particular its coastal towns like Tenby, are in the winter and summer are very different and it is hard to say which Pembrokeshire is the real one. The people of Pembrokeshire then, have many roots and cannot be easily pigeonholed with regards to their lineage - especially compared with other Welsh.

Giltar Headland

2

Pembrokeshire in winter vs in summer: Weird weather, tornadoes and lone lightning clouds

Why? Pembrokeshire peninsula, perhaps

There are two types of working people in Pembrokeshire, those that work in hospitality or those that work for the county council. And that's it. Well, it certainly seems that way. Tenby is a town in which my sweeping generality has much veridicality. The fact that so many people in the county rely on the hospitality industry means the summer months for 'Pembrovians' (a word I just made up that is brilliant) make up a far more lucrative time than do the winter months. The juxtaposition between, say, Tenby in February and Tenby in August is quite something. This also of course applies to seaside towns across the UK -- but the literal distance of Pembrokeshire from urban civilisation (Swansea doesn't count) is marked in the winter compared with other seaside resorts.

Pembrokeshire in the winter, particularly in winters in which it rains often, can be a tad depressing. Oh yeah, it rains a LOT in Pembrokeshire. I remember one year/years when I ran a pub in the village of Lamphey (near Pembroke) in which it rained at least once every day from November to March. I think that was 2016/2017.

That was a rainy few months to say the least, but that kind of inclement weather in the winter isn't all that unusual for the area. Much of Pembrokeshire, after all, makes up a peninsular jutting out into the Bristol channel. The Bristol channel is often cold and rainy and rough and unpredictable, and its weather is our weather all too often. The Atlantic Ocean hugging the western parts of the British Isles also feels the effect of the gulf stream which can have unusual effects on temperature. To experience a 'Pembrokeshire Warbler' weather phenomenon can be to see hail, snow, hot sunshine and then thunder storms all in a weekend. One more thing about the weather in south Pembrokeshire in particular, is that in the winter the snow never really sticks at all. It was a big event as a child to have a rare year in which there was enough snow to scrape off the top of a car to make a snowball -- let alone have enough to make an actual snowman. This again is down to the conditions of a land mass forming a peninsula into a relatively warm part of the Atlantic affected by the gulf stream. Maybe it is this gulf stream that gives Pembrokeshire and in particular the parts of the county forming a peninsular, some weird weather especially in the months where the seasons traditionally change.

WEIRD WEATHER!

One hilarious and terrifying story I remember hearing as an 8- or 9-year-old (around 1990) was told by one of Pembrokeshire's many excellent semi-professional musicians, one of my dad's friends at the time, a chap called Willie. He told me he was in his caravan in Kilgetti (semi-pro pub performing musicians in Pembrokeshire don't tend to live in mansions) and was sat on the toilet doing his thing. He heard a rumbling outside and then a roar that got louder and louder.

He proceeded to arch his neck and look out of his toilet window just in time to see a large black tornado or 'twister' headed straight for his caravan.

Before he knew what had happened his home had been literally turned upside down and he was wearing what had been seconds before, the contents of his toilet. Tornados or 'twisters' as well as sea faring waterspouts are not uncommon in Pembrokeshire. Another thing the locals do not seem to know about but always sort of worried me! Another quite bizarre anomaly in Pembs is that it can have ultra-localised weather conditions. It can be gloriously sunny in, say, Lamphey and in Pembroke just a mile and a half up the road it is dark skies and rain. A recent very weird phenomena I personally experienced happened in the summer of 2020. I was cycling back from Manorbier to Tenby and followed for the 4 or 5 miles one cloud that flashed lightning every few seconds or so for the entire 20 or 30 minutes I was following it. The rest of the sky was blue, sunny and clear. This strange event was filmed by many Pembrovians and appeared on social media the same day, so I know I was not imaging things. It turns out that Pembrokeshire has form with this bizarre phenomenon. In 2013 in another one of those Pembrokeshire no man's lands in between villages a similar occurrence happened to the last one I described. On farmland just between Freshwater East and Lamphey, the farmer of the said land and his neighbour Oliver both saw a quite bizarre occurrence which seems to have had a paralysing effect on all their electrical items.

On a late spring clear evening, both Oliver and the farmer (their properties both being remotely situated in the middle of a field, but about 300 metres apart) heard a repeated crashing sound coming from the land outside. They both came outside at the same time to see what was causing the commotion. Both describe seeing a low-lying single pitch-black cloud firing off bolt after bolt of lightning into the field below! The cloud did not seem to be travelling but just hovering there, angrily zapping away at the ground! Oliver remembers running back into his house feeling it best to take cover and finding all electrics were cut off including mobile phone, the phone landline and internet connection. The farmer described the same thing when he went back to his farmhouse. Oliver described the cloud as looking like Gnasher from Dennis the Menace and Beano fame (anyone under 30 - Google it!).

Pembrokeshire also, in the summer, is one of the few places many people have reported seeing a 'thunder ball', and I just so happen to be one of those people. Luckily, I was with a friend of mine at the time who also witnessed it, so it was definitely real! It was 1996 in Cosheston, near Milton. My friend and I were enjoying a suddenly sunny evening in June, which only hours earlier had been a chilly afternoon. We decided to take our guitars out into the village and our 15-year-old selves had the vague idea of sitting about on the green somewhere and strumming a few tunes in the sun. We walked toward the village church about a half mile away thinking we might plonk ourselves somewhere on the grounds and play some music. Halfway there I noticed the skies had very suddenly become almost dark. It was still warm, but the sky had quickly begun looking angry.

Moments later it absolutely hammered it down with a deluge of warm rain. We ran to a bus stop and took cover. The village pub, the Brewery Inn, was about 50 meters from our position and we both watched an incredibly unusual thing unfold... a glowing red orb like object about the size of a beachball seemed to be drifting downwards from the dark sky. It didn't zip along at all and seemed to be travelling at a steady 30 or 40 mph. We both watched it head straight for the pub. As it did indeed land smack in the middle of the slate roofed Brewery Inn, so it exploded with a massive bang that echoed around the village and made my friend and I jump out of our skin! Something you don't see every day.

With regards businesses, the seasons then in this part of the world affect the surrounds and the lifestyle of the area immensely. Personally, I find Pembrokeshire in the winter a bit of a trial whereas in the summer the county can be a uniquely beautiful place. The landscape of the county with its many beaches and luscious green surrounding landmass can rival the French or Italian rivieras when the sun is shining. The people too (the locals I mean) seem to awaken from May to September. They understand the money to be made in a relatively short period from the pockets of the visiting 'grockels' can make or break a business (the owners) and for the employed staff the long hours of the holiday months can bring in a much-needed consistent wage that is all too scarce in winter. The coming of the spring/summer months change the area and the people. The towns and villages that contain the restaurants and pubs, hotels, B and B's, cafés and shops are bustling with chatter.

Summer sounds in Tenby to me are the rattling of cutlery drawers being opened and closed, the clinking of glasses and the sound of music -- along with a mixture of accents from across the UK. The winter, by contrast, can feel gloomy, insular, and morose. Though doubtless for some there is solace in the county returning in autumn/winter, to its ancient and locally quiet rural aspect. Probably this is truer for those aforementioned types that work for the council and local authorities.

3

Who runs Pembrokeshire?!

Corruption set in centuries

As in other parts of the UK there is often quite a difference in general nature between those working in private industry as with those working for civil authorities in our county. It is known, especially in Pembrokeshire, that these two distinct types see the world differently. Council and local business feuds in Pembs are well known and ongoing. Of course, I am biased coming from a family that ran pubs, but the denizens in positions of real authority in Pembrokeshire county council seem a vapid, interfering bunch, even venal in nature. The stony issue of who gets planning permission in Pembrokeshire can frustrate and point to corruption with many relatively recent large lucrative projects being green lit whilst smaller less obtrusive applications being seemingly arbitrarily refused. More on this later. As many locals will doubtless recognise, my observations here are based in reality. There is a problem between the entrepreneurial type in Pembrokeshire and the bureaucrat. Perhaps this is inevitable, though regrettable, in areas that have two distinct employment options. What can be even more worrying than this, however, is when prominent businessmen and women have excess power within local councils – for obvious reason. This too may be the case in Pembrokeshire especially. Again, the reader has the honour of judgement. Pembrokeshire county council formed in 1996 after the breakup of Dyfed council and the reclassification of authority. Since this time, for a quarter of a century in fact, the council has been run by one party: the 'Independent' party (latterly name changed to the IPPG party). Given that a report by the Electoral Reform Society in 2015 states that one party dominance of any council for 10 years or more is at a roughly 50% higher corruption risk than those with competitive counterparts, the possibility for the strange nature of the PCC one party system becoming a likely venal enterprise can be academically validated. Accusations of corrupt practice involving grant payments have come up often over the years in Pembrokeshire and the Police have had to get involved on more than one occasion. There is no point going too far back so I will highlight a few instances over the last decade where eyebrows have been raised regarding the council's actions. In 2014, a Pembrokeshire Herald article explained one councilor called for more transparency involving a grant scheme, when a local magazine revealed that one property developer Cathal McCosker was receiving the majority of the grants. The magazine christened the property developer as 'the Baron of Bedsits'! The magazine discovered the developments run by McCosker employed one building firm and one local architect's practice to carry out the work. The led to the police investigating the potential scandal. The council has also come under fire on many an occasion over the 'golden handshakes' and seemingly underhand pension schemes some councilors have received. The council came under fire at the time of the said grant investigation when it became public knowledge that a CEO was to receive an enigmatically named 'Pay Supplement' which cost the council, and therefore the taxpayer £45,000! The so called 'pay supplement' was to help this CEO avoid tax on his publicly funded local government pension.

Also, in 2014 an extraordinary attack on PCC by a Tenby councilor Clr. Williams with a text from Clr. Sue Lane set alarm bells ringing for those that had maybe considered the possibility of the misappropriation of public funds by the council. The statement, reported in various local papers read:

> *I'm proud to be a member of the Pembrokeshire Coast National Park Authority but embarrassed to be a member of Pembrokeshire County Council," "The authority is embarrassingly shambolic and the whole set-up is institutionally corrupt. The whole problem is the cabinet set-up which excludes 90 per cent of councillors from decision-making, and as councillors we are starved of information," he continued. Mayor of Tenby, Clr. Sue Lane told Clr. Williams that the town council were concerned that lots of cutbacks had been announced after they had determined their precept and that it was very difficult to budget for the year, with funds for the likes of the gardening services being cut by half and councillors only being 'drip-fed' information. "It's not just the floral side, it's the whole shebang - the furniture, cleanliness and the environmental aspects. It's vital to the economy of the town and we can't afford to let the standards drop," said Clr. Mrs. Lane. Clr. Williams said that towns and community councils across the county were suffering from the cutbacks and that was difficult to comprehend when wage bills at the authority were 'astronomic'.*

In February 2021 it was also revealed that a 'secret deal' to ensure a council member received a £95,000 payoff was protected by a 'gagging order' by senior council leaders to help ensure no 'backbencher' councillor (or anyone for that matter) could speak out against the payoff without inimical conse- quences. Unfortunately, these unwholesome accusations and stories involving Pembrokeshire County Council are not rare.

As I undoubtedly become hated by a large swarth of my county's workforce and now wish I had used a pseudonym, let me continue with an attack on another locally run civil institution – namely the large comprehensive school known as Greenhill. Immediately I will admit that Greenhill did little for me as a student. I left that institution with poor GCSE results and a distinct dislike for authority (Is that coming out in my writing yet?!). However, in later years as a mature student I achieved much academic success at a postgraduate level far away from home. I know I am not the only one with academic promise that feels let down by one of Pembrokeshire's largest educational institutions. That school's department for educational ranking has been awful for decades now. The large school should be a council priority, but it doesn't seem to have improved since I left it 20 odd years ago. When I read the Tenby Observer, otherwise known by many locals as 'the Tenby Disturber', it comes to my attention that the local council is much celebrated, with mayorial changes and pictures of fairly pointless ceremony often clogging up the front page. The obvious council and local business problems are addressed without a serious journalistic edge and smack of cronyism. The poor performance of Greenhill over the years has been skirted over and often ignored. Why should this be the case? Again, I will leave that for the reader to decide.

Returning to strange building applications being cleared, here is an example of small applications and big applications, within metres of each other, being treated by the council differently. My home village of Penally recently (I am writing in 2021) had a building plot cleared for a new holiday homes venture that has quickly bolted on over 40 'homes' (they resemble shacks) onto Holloway field in that village. This multi-million-pound venture by a foreign millionaire businessman without long standing Pembrokeshire ties has essentially created a camp that, from the road, is rather reminiscent of Auschwitz, complete with arched steal gates and road dividing adjacent huts running into the distance. On the other side of the road and 30 metres up, there is a piece of land just next to the Paddock pub. The owners of which have been trying to get permission to build on (one property) since the 90's without luck.

I am sure many reading these words will understand that processes involved in council permission for some controversial building projects in Pembrokeshire could be seen as suspicious. Grange Holiday Homes, Lydstep Bay's transformation from stunning natural space to a 'caravan city', the massive project that replaced the old Fountains Cafe on the Tenby South Beach or even how the once beautiful art deco cinema in Tenby became a gaudy Poundland have raised eyebrows. Despite certain green lit projects that may or may not have spoiled certain spaces in the county, still Pembrokeshire has many unique attractions. The lack of imagination for the advertising of this (mainly) beautiful county on a national level is also a frustrating aspect of criticism that can be levelled at PCC. In fact, the next chapter is dedicated to just that. As an afterthought, anyone that does indeed work for Pembrokeshire county council and suspects corruption can always report it... to Pembrokeshire county council (see sources)!

Holloway Water Bridge

4

Pembrokeshire just doesn't sell it: The hidden in plain sight links to a famous past

The fruits of the chapter before

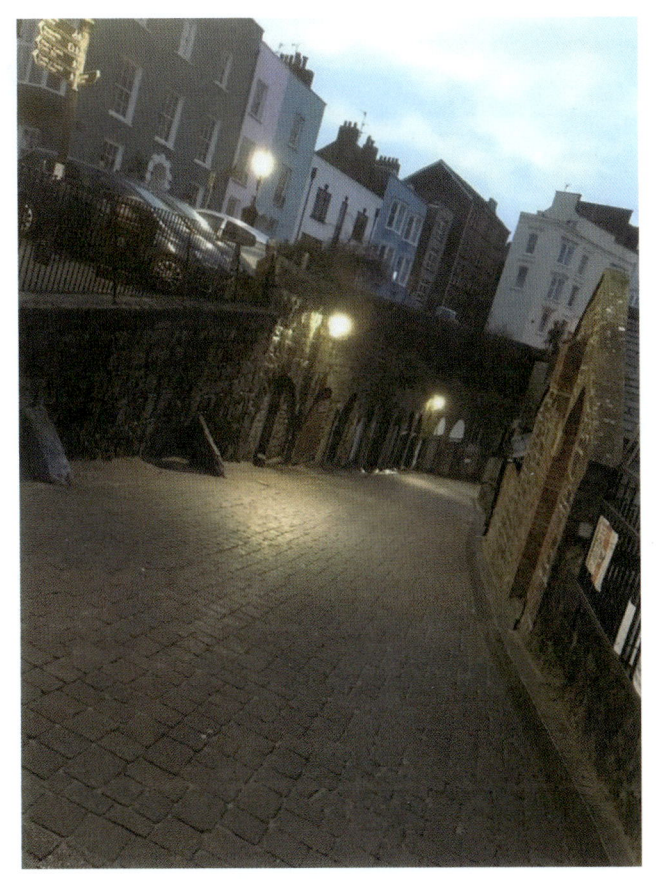

A quiet Tenby evening

Why don't we sell our history better than we do? Why do even many locals not realise what is around them in the county of Pembrokeshire? A myriad of world historically significant links can be traced back to this place. Prehistorically important sites, Celtic royal landmarks, royal dynastic beginnings of earth-shattering importance to the western world as well as scientific and artistic ties to our county are not played up or treasured as they should be.

As I sit here typing and looking out of the window from a lovely vantage point within a house on Penally Heights hill, I can see in the distance the well-preserved remains of a World War One trench network alongside the Pembrokeshire coastal path. This historically significant site carved into the Giltar hills happens to be the last still complete surviving visible trench network used by the British army for practice during WW1 that is left in the UK. It is a vast labyrinth complete with supply and reserve trenches, as well as a HQ trench, all carved into the natural landscape. I suppose the reason I bring this up first in this chapter is to highlight the strangeness of growing up in a Pembrokeshire village as I did, with a site as interesting and significant as this, and yet I did not know about it. Maybe, I hear you inwardly ponder, 'That is because you are uncouth and disinterested!', but no, I was always interested in history. The truth is I knew nobody in my family or among friends that actually either knew about it, or at least if they did, they didn't deem it important enough to advertise the fact it was there. This attitude of disinterest or local ignorance among Pembrovians to their remarkable close history, is I think, unique.

I would say it is vaguely known among many in Tenby that Henry Tudor fled through tunnels under the town to escape his enemies before sailing to France and returning years later to take the crown of England and Wales, but even this is underplayed. The features involved in the actual event are the stuff of legendary adventure, revenge and daring. A tasteful information table explaining the event could be a nice feature for those visiting the town (as you see in many other towns across the country that explain their famous past events). One small blue plaque on Crackwell street with a brief mention of it hardly sets the pulse racing. Tenby councils have form for lack of foresight.

Incredibly, between 1706 and 1781 the powers that be decided to demolish the medieval North gate entrance to the town - it had stood where the Royal Lion now stands. (Tenby town council even got murderous during this period! The mayor of Tenby in 1723, Thomas Athoe, was hanged for the particularly brutal murder of his nephew at Holloway Water. In case you are wondering, Holloway Water is between the Clickets and Trefloyne and can be accessed either opposite Kiln Park Garage (Penally side) or just next to the clickets football pitches (Tenby side). It is a pretty walk. There is an ancient bridge about halfway between Tenby and Penally where the murder took place. In Edward Laws epic history of Pembrokeshire (see source list 10) he asserts that indeed that wicked Mayor does haunt the bridge where the murder took place. When you approach the bridge and pass over it there is indeed a distinctly creepy atmosphere).

Anyway, on with council vandalism… In 1797 the South Gate was demolished and in 1811 the Quay gate also destroyed and removed. A council heavy group at the time known as 'the Corporation' made many of these decisions. Here is the official account of this unfortunate from the Corporation order book as documented in Edward Laws 'Little England Beyond Wales':

> *It is agreed by the Mayor and Common Council of the said Borough that part of the Gate Way the north side of the High Street by projecting into the street is a great nuisance and ought to be removed; it is hereby unanimously agreed that the said Gate Way be taken down, and that a wall be built in lieu thereof in order to make the street more commodious for carriages, &c. ; also that the Town Wall be repaired; also that the stairs or steps to go upon the Town Wall be erected in Frog Street at the north end thereof; and that the said Town Walls be clensed from the Brambles, &c., and made commodious for walking thereon; and that the Bayliffs for the time being be requested to see the same done forwith.*
>
> *Dated the 19th June, 1781*
>
> *H. W. Williams, Mayor, Lawrence Cook, Thomas Voyle, W. Williams, J. Higgon, H. Bevan, John Sayes, Hugh Mountjoy*

Another entry commemorates the evisceration of the great tower on the west wall:

> *January 28th, 1784 — Ordered that a lease of three lives be granted to Michael Morris, of the ground for a Rope Walk from the North Tower to the South Tower in the Whale, for his own, his wife Duence Morris, and John Croade, at the yearly rent of five shillings, to commence from Lady-day next. The breadth at the North Tower to be eleven feet; ten feet at the middle tower, thirty-six feet distance. From the South Gate to be nine feet broad; that he be allowed to make a doorway through the Middle Tower if wanted.*

Laws goes on to mention further vandalism and gives a withering summary in the following passage from the work cited:

> *In the year 18 10 the Quay Gate was taken away, thus leaving only the South-west or St George's Gate. The latter had previously been converted into a powder magazine, which circumstance perhaps preserved it from absolute destruction. Since those days it has been pierced with three additional arches, two of these modern arches knocked into one, and the fabric in 1873 actually ordered to be sold as old material. Actions of this nature when they occurred ninety years ago may be condoned as mistaken utilitarianism, but such deeds if perpetrated now-a-days are rightly designated barbarous folly closely verging on breach of trust.*

During this period of misguided vandalism, it is no surprise to hear that Tenby fell into ruin for the most part, at this time. Charles Norris states in his 1818 work 'Etchings of Tenby", that indeed the period from the later 1700's to the time of 'etchings' so the whole of the south side of Tenby had become as a ruin. Roofless houses and abandoned properties set much of the town's scene. This was the period when pigs ran about the town scavenging for food apparently unowned. It took the benevolent working of Carmarthenshire's William Paxton to put much of this right. With this history of inept councils and poor decision making it seems strange the people of Tenby do not run the town with some form of anarchic system of power by now. Bizarrely well into the 20th century Tenby council also discussed the potential demolition of the Five Arches! It was seriously considered.

Robert Recorde, a figure of immense importance to the worldwide develop- ment of the understanding of mathematics was from Tenby. His farsighted mind led him to be the first person in Britain to accept Copernicus's theory that the earth revolved around the sun. Recorde also introduced algebra to these islands, was the first man to use plus and minus signs in equations, discovered the square root and invented the 'equals' sign! Of course, there is a prominent statue in Tenby to commemorate this giant of the Tudor age, isn't there? Um, no there isn't. Admittedly there is some information on him in St Mary's church and the museum, but his historical importance deserved far more recognition and you cannot help thinking that other towns in the UK would have made far more of such a famous son.

Eight miles further up the road west to Lamphey, Margaret Beauford, the mother of Henry Tudor, lived at the Bishops palace (a now exceptionally beautiful and atmospheric ruin). This history is also not sold as well as it could be. Living in Lamphey as I did for two years and running the local pub, I was surprised by the fact that most locals did not realise the significance of the figure that once lived among their ancestors. Aside being the mother of the Tudor dynasty, Margaret's story is a remarkable tale of a women overcoming extraordinary odds in the cutthroat political world that was English and Welsh medieval patriarchal aristocratic power games. Still, she succeeded, and her offspring would form a dynasty that would change the western world forever when it split the English church ties with Rome in a seismic move by Henry Tudor's son Henry 8th. The Castle in Pembroke also has an incredibly interesting history including its Norman beginning, its birthplace of the Tudor dynasty, its civil war significance as well as its beauty – but once more its importance is not commensurate to its fame nationwide. It was only over halfway through the second decade of the 21st century that the sign for Pembroke on the main road from Tenby was altered to mention the fact that Henry the 7th was born at the Castle in the 15th century. Well done, local government, for only being a mere 5 or 6 centuries late. Finally, also in 2016, a statue of that king was erected at a prominent spot in the town. This, however, is not enough to save the site from its current mediocre look. The town of Pembroke itself is not what it should be. With its historic castle, river and moat the ingredients are there for something that could have been a special destination, but poor town planning has hurt the area's potential. The shops are a steady ramshackle vision incorporating ugly fast-food takeaways, charity shops, far too many cafés, betting outlets (bookies) and, bizarrely, a nightclub smack bang in the middle of the high street. The town could have been rather like a small York or at least a rival to Tenby in its beauty. Instead, the washed up and haggard old high street is without charm. It must be said that there are several interesting businesses that do buck the trend. Main Street music is an excellent port of call for any guitarist in the area. Wisebuys is an excellent outlet for delicious traditional and esoteric foodstuff and Brown's café is surely one of the best places for a traditional fry up in Pembrokeshire – still -- Pembroke's main strip could be so much more. It is interesting as well as disappointing to note that despite the castle's relatively large size, on the road that comprises the high street of Pembroke the castle cannot be seen until you are almost on top of it. Its history is let down by a lack of foresight that predates modern times, maybe. The only clue to Cromwell's epic siege of the castle in 1648 during the second civil war are in the names of some of the pubs dotted about the town. It must be said however that the Castle itself has excellent curators and the tours provided are particularly good. If only the surrounds of the castle were more elegant, and the town planning had lived up to the town's historic past. Once more the fault can only be laid at the feet of the town councils over the ages.

Just a few miles west of Pembroke is another town that could have been so much more. Pembroke Dock boasts the history of a working town with military and industrial importance and pride. Why 'the Dock', as the locals know it, became the rough and ready town it did is much to do with the shipbuilding and manufacturing decline of the UK as a whole. It must be said however, there is still much natural architecture that has not been married with manipulated human design. The potential of the natural features of Pembroke Dock are misused. To put it another way, much of the Dock is a bit of a dump. The docks and marina of the town could and should be invested in and re imagined. Culturally also, this town happens to have played an important role in one of the most successful film trilogies in history. The Millennium Falcon of Star Wars fame was built here. Why there is not a replica of that prop and more made of the Lucas film connection is again a mystery that could easily be rectified, especially since the current manager (2nd in command) of Lucas film responsible for the Star Wars movies is from... Pembrokeshire (Penally)! You cannot make this stuff up! The incredible Millennium Falcon prop weighed all of 16 tonnes and could actually fly! Well, it could hover at the height of about an inch and a half. Still, impressive. The town also boasts (or could boast but doesn't bother) an incredibly interesting and important military instillation. Fascinatingly the fort known as Pembroke Dock's Defensible Barracks was based on Leonardo da Vinci's 'star fort' design and is the last such fortress built along that design in Europe. In 2009 the site was declared the second most endangered Victorian or Edwardian building in Britain.

With its dodgy pubs and partially feral looking populous - instead of a beautiful marina with a Hollywood connection, Pembroke Dock is less Tinseltown and more twin town. Still, at least it has a Lidl.

5

A natural edge, beaufiful landscape, drunk workmen and the lost stone arch of Saundersfoot

Hilarious geological tragedy!

The natural landscape of Pembrokeshire is incredibly ancient. Most of the rocks that make up the county are the best part of 300 million years old. Some rocks that can be found at St David's Peninsula and

the Roch-Treffgarne area are one BILLION years old. Indeed, according to Edward Laws epic 1888 work on the history of Little England beyond Wales, there is nowhere, with the exception of the North American Laurentian and Huronian rock formations, to be found older ground. More recently formed rock that can be found elsewhere in the British Isles are not even represented anywhere in Pembrokeshire. It would seem the very place we walk on here is learned and hardy. There are many examples of faults across Pembrokeshire with a range of different rocks belonging to ancient periods. The north Pembrokeshire Bluestone found at the slope of the Carnmenyn peak is also of course part of the well-known Stone Henge mystery formation - but I think you might have read about that before. From the highest peak in those Hills known as Foel Cwmcerwyn (1760 ft) the insane views include as far north as Snowdonia and as far west as the Wicklow mountain range in Ireland! As well as of historic and cultural value, the geology of Pembrokeshire has given up many rocks of economic value also. Limestone, anthracite (used on Queen Victoria's royal train), slate and sandstone have all been mined in the county over the centuries.

Of purely aesthetic value too, are some of the naturally designed structures dotted around Pembrokeshire. Along the world heritage protected Pembrokeshire coastal walk, immense and beautiful natural rock arches can be viewed and appreciated. One in particular at Stack rocks known as 'the Green Bridge of Wales' is dramatic and framed beautifully from the distance and height of the path overlooking it. There are also smaller natural arches that can be found which are more accessible and that can be appreciated up close. One such an arch existed on the Saundersfoot side of the Wiseman's bridge coastal rock face. This particular arch was unlike anything else around, being of extraordinary diminutive beauty and forming where no such natural feature should have formed. I do not know the ins and outs of why it was so rare, you'll have to talk to some of the older locals that remember it and its visitors. But - my source tells me it was one special arch! People from all over the world came to see this 5-foot mini natural rarity which was well known among geological aficionados. Every summer, visitors (many from as far away as China & Japan) would come to have their pictures taken next to this tiny splendour in Saundersfoot, intricately carved into the coastal stone by millions of years of elemental artistry and pressure.

One summer day in 1974, a work team was building the seawall down there in Pembrokeshire's largest village (The sea wall can still be seen today reassuring those that live on the coast in Saundersfoot). This road crew (about 9 or 10 strong) had been working to create space for foundations to build the new sea wall.

One particular hot summer day work was hard going as they were clearing areas of solid ground stone which incorporated lots of heavy lifting. The five boys on the work crew that were from Pembrokeshire all knew about the arch but had seen it before and it did not hold much fascination for them. On this hot day, lunch time finally arrived, and some of the men decided to trudge to the Wiseman's Bridge Inn to get some lunch. One of the crew, a stout red bearded Irish chap called Patrick (he didn't like to be called Paddy) was well known to the area as he had been a mercenary party to many a Pembs road crew since the early 60s. Patrick was an enjoyer of life and was always happy to walk to the pub at lunchtime. He was one of the numbers that ended up at the Wiseman's Inn that day. Margaret, the landlady at the pub at that time, was fond of the men that made up the road crew as she had welcomed them many times since the sea wall job began two weeks earlier. Margaret always made sure they had some meaty, hardy stew and plenty of homemade bread and butter. Margaret was also happy for them to have a couple of Ales to wash it down with, and she gave them a special rate. This particular lunch went on a little longer than the foreman of the sea wall job, a stern chap from Haverfordwest called Alan, would probably have liked. Fortunately, Alan was having to oversee the beginning of another job in North Pembrokeshire that day and was not due back until tomorrow. Patrick and some of the other men enjoyed more than their usual couple of Ales with the lunch 'hour' lasting from 1pm to around 245pm. Patrick was entertaining some of the local fishermen by arm wrestling several of them one after the other - with the loser having to buy the winner another pint. My source for this story tells me he didn't ever see Patrick lose such a contest.

A little before 3 pm the half dozen or so of the road crew staggered back from the pub and joined the others that had stayed behind and that had had lunch out in the open. The men that did not go to the Wiseman's Bridge Inn were not happy with Patrick and the others and told them they were going to take an extra half an hour break now the pub goers were back so late, because they had been working when Patrick and co had not. Patrick and one of the crew that did not go to the pub, a stocky young chap from Narberth called Dafid, argued heatedly until half the crew did indeed set off to have an extra break to make up the extra time the other half of their colleagues had enjoyed down the pub. Dafid had been in charge of the jackhammer team which had been ploughing a way through the ground stone while others cleared. The aforementioned beautiful arch, he had been warned by foreman Alan the day before, was to be at least 30 yards away from the limit of the digging and was not to be touched for any reason. As he was walking away Dafid thought about this and called back to Patrick, 'And remember! Stay away from that bloody arch'! Patrick muttered a curse back under his breath, 'How dare he tell me what to bloody start with! Who's he to tell me how to do my job'!? A terrible misunderstanding had been set in motion. 'He wants us to start with that bleedin' arch' Patrick growled at one of the crew – one that had himself also enjoyed more than a couple of beers with the pubgoers that lunch time. 'That (hic) funny lookin' arch all the way over there?' said Trev. Trev was an amiable but slightly dim, sunburned young long-haired bloke from somewhere 'up the line'. In fact, all the crew that had gone to the pub that lunch was 'from away' originally. The Pembs boys were the ones that were now off taking their extra break. 'Funny they'd build an arch only 5-foot-high' said Trev as he looked at the geological wonder and began to roll up a cigarette. 'It dunt' even look straight ta' me', muttered Patrick with his deep Wessex brogue. Patrick lit his own cigarette and climbed up some rocks that framed the pristine old arch wonder. He shouted down to Trev to lean the jackhammer against the rock he was standing on so he could reach down and haul it up. Eventually, unsteadily, Patrick stood puffing on his fag above the ancient arch, jackhammer in hand and proceeded to rev up his machine and begin his work. Within three minutes or so Patrick did indeed reduce 100 million years of natural artistry into a small pile of rubble.

Tenby rock formations (St. Catherine's island)

6

Ghosts

Local older entities

I came back from London and decided to walk into Tenby from my home village of Penally. I had arranged to stay at my parents' house. This is an early winter evening, almost dark, early February. I was walking past old Alma cottage and toward the court farm. The crows did that thing they do before they sleep as the sun goes down, when they circle before they return to their nests. An Owl flew over me, bright white and silent. The crows cawed and the sea could be heard distantly in the background. The ghosts that inhabit the villages that make up most of the county are only occasionally active around a soul, but it is usually after immediate transit, after a person returns from a journey. I think I understand the land down here better with time away. The Crows in the village of Penally are in some way of a higher level than other animals. They are instinctively wise; they are also without judgement but are all seeing when active. They sleep and the village sleeps with them. 'Penally crow' is an old epithet for people that hail from that village. Though here the crows are ubiquitous, it was fairly rare to see an owl. Though they could often be heard around the Church late at night.

Walking on another five minutes the Church hove into view, the night fell upon the ground and the outline of the 13th century holy place became numinous. The same ghostly white owl whisked past over me once more and disappeared again into the night. Seconds later two crows also silently zipped overhead apparently separate from the murder that had just gone to their nests. The gravestones almost lean into the old Penally road as you walk past the church. The eyes of a stone angel followed me along the darkening duskily lit road. I felt that even though the only sound that I could hear aside the ever present distant low roll of the sea was of my footsteps, still, I felt something else was about me. As I passed the south side of the church, I felt suddenly compelled to look up the ancient old track toward the entrance of Penally Abbey opposite the east side of the church. What I saw through the dark, cold village air was bizarre and unnerving.

Through a low-lying subtle mist and the silvery weak early night light I distinctly saw what appeared to be three figures that, I am sure, were not expected to be in that place that evening. The central vision was a hooded figure dressed in a pure white shawl or possibly a monk's habit standing at the top of the hill facing me! It was holding up what appeared from my distance away to be a crucifix with its left hand and its right hand was held over its chest. On either side of this strange, hooded figure appeared to be two children, I am not sure as to whether they were girl or boy. They were clothed in what appeared to be dark coloured rags. Each of them was holding out a cup or vessel of some kind, held in both hands outstretched. All three eerie figures seemed to be staring straight at me! I looked away in fright and kept my eyes on the immediate road ahead of me quickening my pace and unsure whether to run. The same two crows swept past me once more and flew into the night. I stole the courage to look back up the road toward the abbey once more, but the figures were no longer there. Suddenly I became very aware of the sound of footsteps seemingly just yards behind me! Then and there my mind was made up about the running. I put my head down and had it away through the village, not looking back. I tore along and suddenly realised, I had got all the way to the Marsh road and was in fact crossing the old bridge where the Ritec river passes under and the place becomes Tenby. I was bent over double on the Tenby side of the crossing exhausted, breathing heavily and at last turned around to look behind me. On top of a telegraph pole just on the Penally side of the bridge, I saw the white owl perched - ethereally lit against the swiftly blackening sky. I also could just make out two crows in an old tree just off the bank of the river, also on the Penally side. I turned and walked on toward town.

It seems there are ghosts in every village and every town in Pembrokeshire. The otherworld plays an important part in the atmosphere of the county at night, when away from the sobering quality of the sea and sky lit daytime. The night in Pembrokeshire does tend to have a spooky quality if you are caught out in it alone for whatever reason. Walking the strange in between no man's lands of ancient pathways and roads that divide villages in Pembrokeshire can be an interesting experience in the evening. Where Lamphey becomes Hodgeston is not entirely clear and I urge the reader to walk that road alone some time, late at night when most are asleep. You will see and hear things that possibly could confound! I know, I have done it a few times when I ran a pub in the area. Back then I would sometimes get insomnia bouts and would head out for a stroll. I still think about the white-haired old lady that passed me at 2.30 am dressed in what appeared through the poorly lit road to be a 1920's era silver frock and high heels. I noticed as she passed by her footsteps made no sound at all. I did not stop and chat.

Some Pembrokeshire ghost stories are quite bizarre. In Carew Castle over the centuries, many people have claimed to have seen the ghost of a Barbary ape! The animal was kept there in the 17th century by Roland Rees, until, it was said, the Ape killed him by ripping out his throat! People claim to have heard a man's screams and the sound of an ape like creature going berserk. That story is fairly well known in Pembs, but another spooky phenomenon attached to the Castle - the mysterious 'ghostly smell' – is less spoken of. To explain, this involves a scent in the castle that becomes overpowering when there is nothing to be seen (stop sniggering at the back). OK, so this is a bit odd - but let me explain. A gentleman I used to know that unfortunately is no longer with us, used to be a stonemason and would sometimes work on ancient Castles and Forts. One day in the early 2000's he was working on Carew Castle. It was in the winter and he was alone in the grounds. Suddenly as he was working on a repair to the North tower, he thought he heard chatter in the grounds below - though he could see nobody. The next thing he knew he was overcome by the smell of cooking meats, breads, cakes as well as the strong stench of mulled wine. He said it was incredibly vivid. He also claims to have tangibly felt the atmosphere of the place itself change from a cold and lonely environment to something he described as 'almost bustling'. To be alone in an ancient castle in the winter and sense those things whilst being seemingly alone must have been odd to say the least. Some days later after explaining what he had felt to the Grounds Manager, he was told visitors to the place have reported this experience often over the years.

An interesting story told to me recently by a local elderly lady, Ann Phillips, who claims to have experienced a bizarre sighting on the Ridgeway road is worth telling. The Ridgeway was an ancient pathway, now road in south Pembs that predates the dark ages. One New Year's Eve in 1969 a young Ann (21 at the time) was working at the Miracle Inn, a glorious old shack like pub in Freshwater East that is unfortunately no longer there (more on this later). Back in the day however the Miracle during summer or on occasions such as New Year's Eve was party central.

The pub was situated in the middle of Freshwater East village and just across the road from the beach. This particular NYE, as 1968 turned into 1969 the party went on a little longer than planned and Ann finally got into her Mini to drive home at 3.15 AM. Ann lived where the Ridgeway road ends, just past the hamlet of Frankleston and just inside the village of Penally, about 10 miles from Freshwater East. Ann left the pub car park and drove up the steep Freshwater East Hill and across dark country lanes onto the Old Ridgeway road. After driving through the village of Lamphey the road goes through no more villages and just cuts through open country all the way to Frankleston and Penally. The road is windy and pitch dark in the early hours in Winter. Ann drove carefully, relying on her trusty Mini to carry her and light her home. As Ann drove past the turn off to Manorbier and slowed for a corner she though she saw in the far distance a glimmer, maybe half a mile ahead. Expecting a car to soon pass she slowed to a steady 30 mph as the Ridgeway is a typically narrow country road. Ann Drove on and then ahead of her the road became straight. She once again saw the glowing object ahead of her. This time however she realised it was stationary. Ann, expecting a broken-down vehicle slowed down to 20 or so miles per hour and dipped her lights. It was so dark with dipped lights she had to lean forward and squint into the windscreen, but she now saw that the object in the road was 100 metres or so away. As Ann got nearer and nearer, she saw to her surprise that the glowing object was smaller than she thought. Ann put her car into 1st gear and drove at walking pace until just yards from the light ahead of her. She stopped the car but kept the engine running unsure what it was she was looking at that was blocking the road ahead. Now however Ann could see that it was in fact a human figure that was emanating light! A sudden fear griped Ann as she realised, she was in the middle of nowhere and alone. Well, aside this thing ahead she was alone. Ann could see the figure appeared to be only around four to four and a half feet tall. She thought perhaps it was a child that was lost, maybe with a torch of some kind but the figure seemed to glow all over. Ann slowly inched her car closer and as far into the side of the road as possible hugging the hedgerow so she could drive by the thing. Ann stared at the figure as she passed and saw that it was the form of a man, it held a spear and shield and was dressed in ancient military attire, breast plate and helmet etc. The craziest thing of all however, its knees appeared to be under the road! It just stood there motionless apparently partly sunk into the very land. Ann, now terrified after seeing what she was sure was a phantom of some kind hit the accelerator and changed up the gears. She drove like the wind all the rest of the way home!

It turns out that many locals claim to have seen 'the Roman' on that part of the Ridgeway...

Another strange story involving my family (Go figure!) with an odd twist relates to another road, namely the Penally bypass. Penally bypass was built in the mid-1960's taking more than a year. The roadcrew all stayed mainly in nearby caravans at Kiln Park or B and B's. The manager of this relatively big project, John, together with his wife Mary rented Truman Park Farmhouse in Amroth. Some Pembrokeshire folk will know that this is the place the well-known Pembrokeshire brick building company Trubloc was conceived in 1946 by Jack Williams. Trubloc of course, taking its name from the farm itself and named by Jack's sister Martha Williams (my grandmother). Trubloc's conception was decades earlier however, and the house was no longer in the family. The project went along very well and soon the vital new road was taking shape nicely. For more than 6 weeks John and Mary were enjoying their new surroundings at the old Farmhouse in Amroth. He would drive off every morning and make sure the bypass was coming along and she would garden the house grounds and drive about the county enjoying the beautiful Pembrokeshire coast and country. One day their peace was to be shattered and new living arrangements had to be made.

On an afternoon after a trip to the shops Mary returned to the old farmhouse and walked through the front door. She found it rather strange that as she stepped through the door the air turned icy cold whilst just outside it was a warm late April afternoon. Mary closed the door behind her entering the hall carrying her shopping. As she walked toward the kitchen door, she heard a creak on the stairs to her left. Looking up she saw a stocky elderly man looking perturbed and dishevelled with unkempt facial hair, a tardy old deerstalker hunting hat and wearing what Mary later described as anachronistic country clothing. Mary froze, later recalling she instantly intuitively knew that this person standing and looking at her from the top of the staircase with a grumpy expression on his face was no longer alive. She dropped her bags and ran straight out the way she came in, slamming the door behind her. She did not ever return to the place. That afternoon Mary met her husband at the worksite and told him the story stating her intention never to go back. John had no choice but to, that very afternoon, arrange new quarters for he and his still shaken up wife. John was lucky to find a Bed and Breakfast just around the corner from the roadwork, at West Holloway Guest house in Penally. That evening John drove back to the farmhouse and packed his and Mary's things whilst Mary settled at her new lodgings at West Holloway. John returned a little later and the proprietors of the B and B made John and Mary a late supper. After, Mary was still a little shaken and sat with John and the lady of West Holloway, the amiable 'Dolly' as she was known, with a pot of tea. They chatted about the road project and how long they intended to stay etc. Finally Dolly asked Mary if she was a little anxious about something and Mary explained what had happened earlier, saying that they had rented a house out in the country. Mary then explained the ghostly apparition she had seen on the stairs. Mary explained she could never go back, also imploring Dolly not to think she was crazy, that something like this had never happened before. It was Dolly's turn to feel a little nervous now.

'Your description of the old gentleman sounds a lot like my late father!' said Dolly. Dolly explained he had also often worn an old deerstalker hunting hat and was not one to exhibit a pristine appearance.

'I'm sorry if that reminded you in a sad way about your father,' returned Mary. 'I suppose many country folks wore similar clothing'.

'Tell me,' asked Dolly, 'where was this country house?'

'It's a place known as Truman Farmhouse in Amroth,' said Mary and took a sip from her teacup and put it back on its saucer on the table.

'Dolly', or to give her an official title, Mrs. Martha Phillips -- formally miss Martha Williams, suddenly reached forward and grasped poor startled Mary's hands.

'That was the house I grew up in!' She exclaimed before releasing Mary and reclining back into her chair.

Martha, John and Mary sat quietly stunned for a full minute, with the ticking of the carriage clock on the shelf keeping a tempo for the silence.

7

North Pembrokeshire

A tangible delineation within the whole

I am sure that it will not have escaped the attentive reader's notice that I have mainly written about South Pembrokeshire and have not thus far paid attention in a serious way to the North of the county. This then will be a chapter solely dedicated to North Pembrokeshire. Reading over what I have written so far, I accept that it is possible for an unconscious or at least an unintended favouritism to have affected my writing and so I have possibly overrepresented the South in this work. It must be said there is an unfortunate distrust between those of the North and South of the county. Unfairly it has been believed by some that the South Pembrokeshire person looks down at what they feel to be the less sophisticated and more insular northern Pembrokeshire person. I aim to write dispassionately and factually about the North, and I will not allow my southern allegiance to interfere with a fair representation of that place. I feel I am qualified to write about the area with authority, as I have visited North Pembrokeshire at least three times.

Pembrokeshire is officially one county, although as everyone from these parts knows very well, unofficially, the north and south of the county are completely different places. I did touch on this in chapter one, but that chapter explained these differences from the perspective of the South only. Let us now journey across the northern border of the Landsker line and delve into what is to us from the South, a strange and foreign land and culture.

The first thing to note about the North is the mysterious language spoken up there. It is a form of Welsh that has not been communicated anywhere else in Wales since around the 13th century. It is illegal to speak any language other than Welsh in North Pembrokeshire ('new Welsh' is permitted). This offense, known as 'diafol siarad' loosely translating as 'devil speak' carries a stiff jail sentence. Anyone caught speaking English in the north of the county can expect an expedited trial without legal representation and summary execution. The method of execution for the crime of 'ceg bradwr', loosely translated as 'traitor mouth' is too brutal to write about in an accessible book such as this bearing in mind children and those of a sensitive nature may be reading.

Despite the many old fashioned and traditional values that are still important in North Pembs, there has been a hi-tech revolution of sorts in recent years up there. Almost 65% of dwellings in North Pembrokeshire now have both hot and cold running water. Also, since the great 'open hand' policy implemented by the mystic elders of the county in 2008, there has been great uptake in land line instillation as well, with almost 35% of houses now having a telephone installed. Telephone engineers that visit the county, or 'dyn hud trydan' as the locals call them (again, a loose translation to English - 'an electric magic man') are revered and treated well when they visit the area. In 2016 North Pembrokeshire's library had three almost new Internet connected computers installed with a ceremony involving the local elders blessing the machines with smoke from burning sage and performing the 'dawns y dylwythen deg' or 'dance of the fairy' in celebration.

Culturally also, the North has made progessive steps in recent years with the elders of the mystic council (to give them their full title) permitting the practice of non-pagan ritual on private land. Children are benifitting also from new open-minded cultural policy in NP. At schools, as from 2019, the teaching of things 'y tu hwnt i dir y ddraig' or 'beyond the realm of the dragon' is allowed once a week on a Friday by a specialist teacher (albiet with elders overseeing the lesson). Nations around the world and their strange religions, cities and landscapes are tentatively described and explained to open mouthed children. Children that until recently knew the world only as far as the borderlands of Ceridigion and the southern Pembs Landsker dividing line. These lessons involve the 'ways of the outside' and have even begun to enlighten students in North Pembrokeshire on the Galilein heliocentic vision of the solar system; which since the 1970's had been accepted by the elders - but not passed on to the everyday folk -- until now.

The 1990's scandal involving the mysterious disappearance of several visiting councilors from South Pembrokeshire is almost forgotten with the onset of a fresh new inclusive paradigm from the mystic elder council of the north. The rumours surrounding the disappearance of the three said senior South Pembs councilors in 1997, regarding cannibalism, have never been substantiated. Indeed, there has not been any real evidence of ritual cannibalism in north Pembrokeshire since the mid 1980's. Unfortunately plans for a future delegation from South Pembs councilors to visit their colleagues in the north have been put on hold several times. A mysterious illness striking the would-be diplomats, incredibly on the eve of all previous dates, has delayed a visit. Pagan ritual is still important to the people of North Pembrokeshire, but much previously common state-sponsored superstitious public practice has been scaled down. Also, 'Wicker Man' type fiery human sacrifice to assuage the Gods and bring luck to future harvests is almost a thing of the past in the north of the county. Human sacrifice, though not strictly illegal in North Pembrokeshire, is certainly looked down upon these days by many of the people north of the Landsker. Witch doctors and shamanic ritual and herbal remedy are still the prevalent form of practice for the amelioration of sickness, but some modern medicine including paracetamol, aspirin and antibiotics can now be obtained with special license. Progression in North Pembrokeshire is certainly on an upward curve.

Despite these undoubtedly impressive open-minded changes politically, scientifically and culturally in the north, there is still much distrust for those in the south of the county. The south of the county is still known up north as 'tir maip gwenwyn' or 'the land of poisoned turnips'. This disparaging sobriquet reflects the unfortunate still contemporary dislike of the South. Maybe things can change for the better very soon and trust between us can be won. I hope to have at least done my bit by advertising in this book, the impressive progressive steps taken by the North in recent years. I would like the South Pembrokeshire reader to understand they are quite human up there, just like us and should not be feared (providing when visiting you stringently follow local laws and customs). I hope that if this work is one day published in medieval Welsh, then the northern Pembrokeshire folk will learn that we are friendly and welcoming down here and have the utmost respect for their ways and values.

8

Picking up in Pembrokeshire - a guide to stepping out

Going 'out' out

Who dares wins, right? It is time to head out into the hit and miss world of chatting up the ladies in a Pembrokeshire town. I'm going to go with Tenby again as it is a town I have been shot down in flames and crash landed in many times when I've been a single man and in the county. Also, they say to write about what you know -- so this section will be from the perspective of a heterosexual man, between 25 and 45, aiming to secure phone numbers or even coitus from the local or visiting ladies. I am sure however, some of the points I will make about Pembrokeshire/Tenby dating could go for ladies looking for gents or girls for girls/boys for boys also. Anyway, as I was saying, my perspective is from a man seeking Local OR visiting ladies... this brings me to the next point that must be made. Well, due to the juxtaposition of Pembrokeshire in holiday season and when without of it, then the first thing to ask is, are you trying to pick up locals or those from 'up the line'? The second option is probably out during the Winter.

Winter dating in Pembs

Going out and looking for action in my home town in the Winter is a tricky affair. Tenby's winter population is around 5000. Probably, you will only be interested in the sex of half of those. Then, when you take into consideration that a third of the population of Pembrokeshire are over 55 -- about another quarter under 20 -- suddenly your sheer numbers are being whittled down alarmingly quickly. Another factor to consider is that most women falling within those ranges in Pembrokeshire that are sane and have their own teeth are normally married with children. Suddenly then, the options 'on the pull' in Tenby out of season get limited (see the next chapter to explore Pembrokeshire dating variables even further). Let us not let that put you off. There ARE eligible ladies out there -- I have definitely seen at least four of them around in the recent winter months. Ok, so...What should one wear in Tenby in the winter on a Saturday night whilst on the lookout for romance? Well, winter in Tenby can be bloody freezing when there is a northerly wind, and it is raining - as it probably will be. But, as explained in an earlier chapter, it will not snow, so do not worry too much. Still, take a good heavy jacket/coat, possibly with gloves and maybe a hot water bottle. Oh, and a woolen hat. Also, before you dress, rub some deep heat on your chest, arms and legs to be on the safe side. Oh, and do bring an umbrella.

Ok, so you are dressed and ready to hit the town. February in Tenby is a little quiet. Still, you and a couple of other single friends head out in hope. Where do you go? Well, about half of the pubs, it seems, are not open. You head to the 'Tenby Triangle', that triumvirate of public houses that comprise The Lifeboat, the Tenby House and the Buccaneer. At last, you see one or two people milling about outside the Tenby house and go there first.

Unfortunately, the people you saw from a distance were just, in fact, door staff (there are always too many outside the TH). It soon becomes clear after entering this establishment (after you have addressed the shock of the too loud dance/shite dated club music) that the staff outnumber the customers. Suddenly you notice that one of the barmaids is your ex from years before. Before you know it you and your friends are sitting at a table together with slightly flat winter beer, barely able to hear each other speaking. Also, you are getting evil eyes from an ex that hates you and one of the bigger doormen was from your year in school 20 odd years ago and he was someone you didn't ever talk to and he probably thinks you're a bit of a stuck-up dick. Also, he is the boyfriend of your ex behind the bar, you know, the one that hates you. After drinks in all three Tenby Triangle rubber dubs there is a vague bit of flirting from a table of girls in the Lifeboat and a determination is made by you and your friends to go on to a late licence bar. After all, there may be more where this came from with the same idea in Tenby tonight, even though the ratio of men to women looks to be an absolute festival of bratwurst over the fairer sex.

Where do you go after 11 pm in Tenby to carry the night on? I think many locals reading this will feel a chill run down their spines as the royal title of the first-born son of the monarch comes lolloping into their minds. Yes. The Prince of Wales... According to Christine Willison, author of Pembrokeshire Folk Tales, there are three places you can see the otherworld or begin a journey to the other world from in Pembrokeshire - those being Pen Cemaes, Narberth and Cym Cych. May I suggest to Christine she can quite confidently add the Prince of Wales in Tenby to this list. Probably there is a late-night club like it in every provincial town. The Prince of Wales is situated on Frog Street and has been providing Tenby locals, all year round, but especially in winter, with all manner of regrettable opportunities that are often realised on a regular basis. Waking up with the infamous black smudged stamp from the Prince of Wales (or Prince of Darkness, giving it its popular local sobriquet) on your hand (given as you pay and enter the club) is confirmation that those things DID happen the night before. That indeed, the girl lying next to you in some strange bedroom that smells of damp and vomit, is in fact not a hallucination, she is indeed there. And yes, it IS your ex that served you last night in the Tenby House that sleeps beside you. Also, there is a text from a friend on your phone telling you that 'Darren' (the large doorman boyfriend of the said girl) has already heard about it and wants to 'kick your head in'.

Summer dating in Pembs

As opposed to winter in Tenby, summer in Tenby, particularly when the weather is good is a bustling and busy scene. We will get to the 'bucket and spade' daytime Tenby at some point in another chapter (maybe), but now I want to talk about 'Summer Tenby' late night. A time when the ladies and gents are out in force, and aside the 15-year-old local lads trying to get in the pubs with fake IDs, all children have long since retired to their caravans and tents at Kiln Park.

The pub scene at night in Pembrokeshire towns during mid-summer can be an eventful folly. A typical night's build up can be calm and deceiving. The early evening post 6pm vibe in Tenby during a warm summer can be very pleasant. Crimson faced families make their way slowly through the town slightly drunk on ice cream and sunshine and back toward their holiday bases. In hotels dotted around town, girlfriends are having a glass of sparkly stuff, laughing and dancing in pre-evening holiday getting ready to go out parties as they change into evening wear. Local fishing gentlemen are just finishing work down the harbour and popping to the Hope and Anchor for a swift one that may indeed turn into more than a swift one. The smell of chips and vinegar mixed with David Beckham aftershave, Jimmy Choo perfume and Lynx Africa drifts into the relaxed milieu. A pub door is heaved open and for a few seconds Peter Andre can be heard crooning 'mysterious girl', before the door swings closed again. Seagulls are mopping up the Greggs and Fecci's detritus sprinkled along the streets and they caw and fight each other for prizes. The night is young and full of promise. Trains are speeding toward Tenby from the South Wales Badlands with many a can of Stella and Dark Fruits cider being quaffed and staff in pubs and bars around Tenby gear up for the second part of their 13-hour shifts. After 8pm summer Tenby can become loud and excitable. Live music from one of the many hit and miss live acts that live and perform in the area (the 'hit' ones can be excellent) can be heard in several pubs, and loud 'club' like music in others. As a local going out into the wild Tenby air of a summer night in search of love or even just something more casual you need to remember a couple of things. Sure, there are many more options out there than in the non-seasonal months, but there are many more self-preservation kinds of things to keep in mind also.

The type of lady 'from away' frequenting the bars about town in the summer can be quite a handful. Some of them, particularly our friends from the South Wales valleys can act like will o' the wisp type spirits that can lure you into danger. Dressed in their best leopard print frocks and new look 'fuck me boots' these femme fatales can be an alluring new element for the romance starved local, despite their often-ample size. It is surprising what can begin to attract in a starved land. As the Israelis say, 'in the desert, every thorn is like a rose'. The swamp lands these particular thorny women often amuse themselves luring you into are patrolled by their male counterparts. Whole towns and villages from 'up the line' seem to head out into the Tenby night together and their loyalties lie still in Merthyr Tydfil,

Llangenech and Neath. Local men can often be seen in summer ill-advisedly attempting to chat to a table, seemingly of girls only, thinking that their luck is in. Many rounds of Cider and black, garish cocktails and Sambucca shots can be purchased by naive local lads thinking that the investment is surely worth it in the coming hours. There is unfortunately, inevitably, the arrival of 'Gaz', 'Mad Huw' and 'Big Dave' -- just when it all seemed to be going so well... For the persistent and brave local lad in Tenby this time of year however there are spoils to be had -- it takes sticking together with your crew and understanding when it all seems too good to be true and moving on.

9

Online dating in Pembrokeshire

Scoring with satellites

Tell me when! Will I see you again!?

Well, in most cases no. Online dating in Pembrokeshire is hilarious. The lack of southern or Western county border as well as the limited population make things more difficult and restricted for the would-be Pembrokeshire online Romeo or Juliet. Given that the entire relatively large county space has just 126,000 or so people within it, and the fact that within that number (again assuming that many people are interested in one sex only) only half are the correct sex to be considered, options become relatively scant when other realistic 'ruling out' factors are considered. The number of suitors of the correct sex that is left is then (assuming the person using the app is sane) greatly reduced by factors including age, attractiveness, distance etc. This means that any discerning suitor will have only a handful of possible matches to choose from in an area slightly larger than London. Shall we break it down using simple common-sense assumptions?

What follows may not appear to be using completely accurate scientific methodology and admittedly not researched at a forensic level but hear out what I have to say and see if you agree with me just a little bit . . .

OK. Let us say I am a single man, wishing to find a girlfriend in my home county of Pembrokeshire. I download an app on my phone and begin to look through what is available. Before we even start to break down what is suitable it must be said that 17% of Pembrokeshire's population are below the age of 16 and another 25% are over the age of 65. Let's assume we can rule out those last bracketed age groups (one or two Greenhill teaching staff past and present would probably bemoan this sensible act but that is a whole other story). Now you are left with maybe 70,000 people. Now, as I said, assuming you are interested in one sex only that figure now becomes 35,000. Ok, still. Sounds not too bad right?! How many of those are actually single and available? Let's be optimistic and assume 70% are indeed single. OK, so now we are left with about 25,000. How many of those 25,000 are actually on online dating? Let's be generous and say half of them are using an app, then we are left with about 12 or 13,000. So, next the app will, naturally, ask which age group I would consider. Let's assume I take an age group within a suitable number of years to my own age. If I'm 35, I'd probably be looking at the part of the 13,000 left that are between the age of, say, 25 to 40. The online dating number of possible suiters left within the bands of my age selected takes that 13,000 figures to somewhere in the region of less than half that. Let us say then, we're left with 6,000 (unlikely!). How many of those are using the same app as you?

Let us then say 5000 are. OK. 5000 possible suiters... not bad right? However, how many of the (probably way too high 5000 number) potential dates that are left do you actually fancy – that is – that you would swipe right for/send a message to? Let us be EXTREMELY generous considering it is Pembrokeshire we are talking about and say that you would 'fancy' every 1 in 5 – that would leave about 1000. Next, a very, very important factor has to be considered: How many of that (almost certainly inflated figure) 1000 will fancy you back and swipe right for/message you?

Speaking as a man in decent enough shape that hopefully would not scare the horses, I would guess that if I used an app such as Tinder, I might get a one in 10 success rates of responses (who I like, like me back). That 1000 number is now 100. Let us now assume that I have been quite generous all the way through this section and realise that that 100 number is more like 80... Well... that 80 potential partners are also getting 'matches' and messages from their 80 possibles, not just you. Let us also not forget that a man needs to know girls get more 'matches' than men for myriad reasons, so they are likely to have even more than 80 possible suitable matches. Let us now say that for each of that 80 left you have a one in 10 or so chance of actually securing a date, before all of the other 80 plus men she is talking to. Suddenly that 126,000 population of Pembrokeshire – if you are looking to see how many of them you really want to/could potentially date using the online method, in say, a period of a year -- comes down to a population of less than 10. That is, maybe, 5 to 10 that you will 'fancy' and they will fancy you back. That you have a chance at dating -- if you are lucky and manage to get them between other dates! As stated, chances are also relatively high that these few potential partners will be an ex-partner of someone you know . . .

Using an online dating app, I have been told, in Pembrokeshire, will throw up the same people even after your online 'rejection' has been implemented as there just are not enough people to go around. The app will basically cheat you and keep spitting out the same faces. As many people in key Pembrokeshire towns will understand, much bad feeling has come about with many people dating their friend or acquaintance or colleague's ex-partner - due to the limited options available to a far distant rural county such as is Pembrokeshire. One ridiculous story (I will change the names involved) happened to a friend of mine summer 2020. I was travelling to a supermarket in Haverfordwest with my friend, Sam.

Sam had matched with a girl called Sarah and showed me her picture. I realised I had dated her in my late teens. I wasn't bothered so didn't tell Sam. However, Sam then realised with a late epiphany that Sarah was in fact the same Sarah that was his boss's ex-fiancé. We were laughing about this as Sam parked his car in the store carpark. Suddenly there was a tap on the window that made us both jump. It was Sam's boss (the one who'd dated Sarah) who just happened to be walking past the carpark as we drove in and came to say hi! Then, after his boss went on his way we went into the supermarket. As we are queuing to pay for our beers and crisps who should be in the line just in front of us? Yes, that's right. Sarah. There was an awkward moment as Sarah and Sam clocked each other realising they had matched online dating. They sort of gave each other a knowing smile and Sarah scuttled off. Pembrokeshire in its entirety is not so much of a 'small world' but rather more like a 'large small town'. Sam and Sarah, I am sad to report, did not actually ever arrange that first date.

Online dating with limited choice in small counties with peninsulas, especially one like Pembrokeshire with no south or western border counties, can, and does cause all manner of distrust and antagonistic behaviour to manifest. It is just so difficult due to the restrictive geography and population to meet anyone that does not already have some connection to you already. Whether it be that they may have dated someone you know or that they know someone you previously dated. I am sure the apps available have brought many people together over the years down here. I would be betting though, due to the difficulty of practicing discretion in Pembrokeshire, and their ease of use, they may also have helped to end many relationships as well.

10

Where did all the cocaine come from?

Not to be sniffed at

There has been more trouble than there should be on the streets of Tenby in recent summers. Without pointing the finger solely at our friends from South Wales it does seem like they are responsible for more than their fair share of the unfortunate fighting and crimes involving assault that are no stranger to Tenby in seasonal months. Another issue certainly relating to all this is the relatively recent inimical upsurge in cocaine use in the UK that Tenby has not escaped, and in fact has been affected by more acutely than most other towns around the country. This is because Tenby is on one of the new drug routes from London and on to Ireland by land and is susceptible (Pembrokeshire as a whole) to more recent sea smuggled drug landings in ports like Fishguard and Milford Haven. The now popular drug smuggling sea route out of West Africa has also undoubtedly used the quiet county of Pembrokeshire and its lightly policed sleepy ports as an end point over the last decade. In very recent years there have been persistent rumours in Tenby that some businesses in the town have been bought out by elements from the major cities with unwitting local management brought in to run the 'legitimate' businesses. These premises are then used for money laundering as well as drug distribution hubs for Tenby and for the routes on to Ireland and especially the city of Dublin. When recently I studied an Organised Crime module in London for an MA, our lecturer

Produced a map of well-trodden drug routes out of the capital to provincial areas. Tenby was at the end of one such a route. However, it has happened it is true that the upsurge in cocaine use in Tenby over the last decade by locals as well as those visiting, has increased the risk of violence and addiction down here. In the summer months in a town like Tenby that relies on nightlife and the buying of alcohol that goes with the territory of a coastal town in the season, a cocaine surge cannot do any good. Police numbers in Tenby during peak season have never really been sufficient to deal with the binge drinking related violence. Add to the overstretched copper's woes the extra problems that come with a new cocaine epidemic and there is clearly a big issue to deal with in the coming years.

A few years ago, I was surprised whilst visiting for a weekend night out in Tenby after some time away, at just how hyper it all got after 9 pm. The tell-tale wide eyed and overly chatty antics of many locals I knew told me that this drug had become readily available in the town. Doing a little research into this I found that, putting the health risks to one side, the purely economic factors for one using, particularly in a provincial town like Tenby, were as high as the users. Tenby prices it seems - let us say for a gram of cocaine - are far in excess of what you would expect to pay in London (about 30% to 50% higher). In recent years, a few people I know have had the drug on them whilst I have been out and about with them. After checking the product available in Tenby, it seems quite obvious to me that the 'cocaine' available this far from civilisation has in fact been 'stepped on', probably several times. The availability of the drug 'any time anywhere' in Pembrokeshire has become realistic with smartphone technology.

Last summer (2020) I was having an early Tuesday evening beer at a pub in Penally. It was great to see some old friends about my age (30's and 40's) that I had not seen for years. These are mates that have not really left Pembrokeshire's comforting bosom too often over the years and are in decent steady blue-collar jobs, etc. All of them I met that night have children, even teenage children. The evening in question was a very sunny and comfortable 18 or 19 Celsius with clear blue skies. As was in the old days, once some of us Penally Crows got together after a long time without meeting, so plenty of imbibing would commence. Within an hour (and don't forget this is a Tuesday 'school' night) I begin to realise at least a couple of the table were not just enjoying their pint and a cigarette. On a table of six or seven of us it turns out three of my friends were using cocaine. One of them was running low and ordered a one gram 'wrap' then and there on a secure messenger app. My friend contacted his 'dealer' and deposited the £80 charge into a bank account. Then, 30 minutes later he strolled off down the road and within moments was back at the table. This isn't a 19-year-old getting supplied ready for a Saturday night out on the town, maybe to hit a club later. No. This was a man with a family and with work the next morning. His behaviour, at least to himself and the others at the table was not particularly out of the ordinary. It certainly appears as if cocaine use has become far more 'normalised' in Pembrokeshire than it probably should be.

Despite the cons involved with using cocaine in small town Wales, so the market for it appears unsated. I am certain many of the readers (especially younger local readers and business owners) will know these things to be true. On a positive note, to end this chapter I will say this problem is not unprecedented down here. I remember in the late 1990's there was a similar surge in cocaine use in the area which was in the end dealt with – largely by people becoming aware of the problem and business owners/police getting their collective acts together. In terms of the police, perhaps pointless busts on poor people's houses in estates around the county just to confiscate someone's bit of weed/hash could be put on the backburner. Instead, resources could be used to target local gangsters and dealers peddling coke. I'm certainly not one to judge one way or the other about the morals involved with drug taking, but in my experience, cocaine is often conducive to twattish behaviour. The odd 'cheeky line' here or there is harmless enough for some people, but when the use of it becomes chronic the downsides for the user and the poor sods around him/her become overwhelming. Cocaine is a drug that can make nice people turn selfish and has the power to turn someone that is already a bit of a dickhead into someone unbearable. Its extraordinary cost can tear into family incomes with all the misery this can cause (increasingly the middle aged are becoming chronic users). It also tends to make those with an already violent disposition into an even more dangerous person. I hope Tenby finds a way to make it less of a problem than it undeniably is today. Tenby, as I said, has sorted it before, I'm sure it can again.

11

The 'Lost Worlds': Licensed premises that are legend in Pembrokeshire (my selecfion)

The glorious lost watering holes

Fancy a pint?

here were a number of pubs and clubs in our county that are no longer of this earth but have left so many memories. It would be foolish of me to attempt to list them all so I will limit my chapter to several that I feel most people in the area (30 years plus maybe) still talk about. The Bryn Hir will be remembered by readers of a certain age. My knowledge of that place has been passed down from several older friends of mine. Imagine a pub/club on the outskirts of Tenby where one could have a quiet pint in the afternoon, watch live music in the evening, then graduate to a late-night disco which could go on until breakfast time! THEN, at 7am or so, you could order a fry up with a cup of tea! I wish it had still been going in my late 90's heyday in Pembs, when, as now, the best to offer after 11 PM without travelling too far from Tenby was the dreaded Prince of Wales. I say dreaded Prince of Wales, but I, as well as you reading this will undoubtedly end up there again someday, I'm sure.

Another pub mentioned briefly in an earlier chapter was the aptly titled 'Miracle Inn' once in the coastal village of Freshwater East. When first laying eyes on this place you would have to think, 'It's a miracle it's still standing!'. Essentially, the Miracle was a large wooden shack – it was only meant to be a temporary structure - but it stood from the mid-1960s until 2000's. It started out life as 'the Golden Sands Restaurant and Freshwater East Club'. Essentially it was a limited member's club with gambling etc. The management there - George and Colette Bethwaite - applied for a 'full on' license for the premises but privately held out little hope of it being granted. In those days the council wasn't often handing out new license status' to places in Pembrokeshire. The Bethwaites believed it would indeed be a miracle if the license was granted. When, against all odds it was granted, there could only be one name for the new pub.

The Miracle Inn was a funny old place. It was situated next to swampland and its kitchen staff had to be constantly mindful of the large water rats that would continuously (often successfully) try to invade the pub at night. The 'shack' had two sides to it -- one a traditional enough looking pub and the other more like a bar with a dancefloor. The carpet of the pub side had never been changed by the end of The Miracle's 30 odd year run. As you walked in during the pub's later years you could see vague pathways trodden into the old material on the floor that had been formed over decades. The smell was like being in an old damp caravan after someone had spilled a bottle of wine on the floor and then tipped into the spillage an ashtray full of lambert and butler butts. The 'disco' or live room side of the structure comprised one large open space with a bar at one side and a stage and DJ booth on the other. Most of the space in that room was taken up by an old wooden dancefloor that got so sticky in the thrall of Saturday night fever that people's shoes would often stick to the floor when dancing and come off. The Miracle Inn was situated at the bottom of one of Pembrokeshire's longest steep hills and about a 90 second walk from the beach. It was one of those places easier to arrive at than leave. Many late-night parties at the pub, rather than facing the chore of walking home would end up on the beach. Many reading this of a certain age may well remember a story connected to a night out at The Miracle Inn, I am sure.

In its early days of the 60's and 70's it was one of the live music venues that somehow managed to attract some very well-known and respected names. The roll call of bands that would head to The Miracle Inn may surprise some. Here are just a few: Amen Corner, Dave Edmunds, Billy Fury, The Merseybeats, Gerry and the Pacemakers and Hot Chocolate. There are many more, but I am sure you get the point. I'm also told by a reliable source - a former manager of the pub in the late 70's -- that in fact, Mark Knopfler also performed an impromptu drunken acoustic gig at The Miracle just before embarking on Dire Straits first European tour in 1978.

Imagine a place now in Pembrokeshire, where you could go see a big band at such an exciting but no-frills venue as was The Miracle. Unlike the contemporary Queens Hall in Narberth, which while having some excellent more esoteric folk/blues acts and tribute acts etc, the Miracle really did get some of the biggest original names in Pop and Rock.

Historical musical tragedy is also connected to the place. Dickie Valentine, a big star in the 1950's played his last gig at The Miracle Inn. Valentine had had two number ones and many top 10 hits in the UK (including the UK's first Christmas number one single). By the 1970's he was touring in smaller venues around the country but still attracted a following. In May 1971 after performing at The Miracle, Valentine and the other two members of his band at that time (Sidney Boatman and Dave Pearson) were driving to their next gig in Caerphilly. It seems Dickie lost control of his vehicle at high speed on the way, and all three in the car were killed. Dickie Valentine was just 41, Sidney Boatman and Dave Pearson were 42.

After The Miracle Inn's heyday of the 1960's and 1970's, the 80's and 90's saw the pub became a popular venue for local talent. In its later years, its clientele were a varied bunch and the summer atmosphere at the pub was always zesty and fun. Surfers would frequent the place as well as German Army personal (Castle martin Tank regiments mainly), musicians, locals and 'bucket and spade' holiday makers. All would mingle without trouble (chilled beach shack that it was) and get drunk together. There were always interesting comings together at The Miracle, with loud conversation and dancing and the jukebox or live band blasting away hits in the background. Future Welsh Rock Star Euros Childs, lead singer of the future Gorky's Zygotic Mynci would hang out at the pub during its later era. He would go on to name his 2007 solo album 'The Miracle Inn'. Unfortunately, by that point the once great pub and venue were gone. In that album's title song, 'The Miracle Inn', some of the lyrics remind me of my time as a child living at the pub (my parents ran it from 87' to 91' -- part of the time Euros is writing about). Childs sings 'Just a shack by the beach, with peeling back paint, but it meant so much to me'. However, as Euros goes on to say in the song, 'Now the place is a car park, and now when it gets dark, I know I can't get back'.

A cool looking couple, having a pint at The Miracle, sometime in the 80's

Another equally legendary nightspot (which is still there but in different form and not in its old late-night club incarnation) was Chequers. Ah Chequers! Chequers was (is) just in between Penally and Lydstep. I remember having my first beers there as a wide eyed 14-year-old, with the Whigfield cheesy club classic 'Saturday night' blaring away in the background! Back then in Chequers (94' ish) it was the place to go as an underage youngster for weekend late night fun. It seems incredible thinking back to then that its license was not taken away long before it eventually was in 1997. I always remember the Friday nights at that place -- £5 on the door to get in and then 50 pence a bottle of Bud all night! There was always an insistence to see a fake ID as you went in. It didn't matter how obviously fake the ID (I think my 14-year-old mug was attached to a card that proclaimed I was a 'truck driver' on a fake company name I had made on the school computer) just as long as you showed something.

Drug dealers would walk about the club openly offering their wares. As I remember it was generally speed, pills or, bizarrely, acid tabs! Quite why someone would want to head to a provincial nightclub full of school kids, Pembroke Dock hard men and travellers - and then drop acid - is beyond me. But people did. The place always had the slight feeling of menace and edge due to amphetamine use, cheap booze and the local rivalry between the area's tribal entities. The fights in there would spill out into the road outside and they were seemingly every weekend. Milford Haven's finest would take on stationed 'squaddies' from away. Pembroke boys and Tenby boys would duke it out and the travelling community from about the area would take on everyone! It was quite the education for a 14 or 15-year-old to see all that we saw in that club back then. One of my strangest memories was of myself and a couple of friends sitting at a table when a couple at a nearby booth started having sex. I mean the whole shebang. She just climbed on top, and the ultimate public quickie happened right before our amazed teenage, until recently, innocent eyes. No doormen stopped them, and it seemed to go on for about five minutes or so. I seem to remember Urban Cookie Collective's club hit 'I've got the Key; I've got the Secret' was blaring out as they went at it.

The drug thing eventually got so big there that they tell me on the night in 1997 that it was finally busted, the dance floor was completely covered in wraps, pills, strips of acid, and baggies! People saw the police bursting in and the panicking mass tossed the lot. Somebody somewhere must have a picture of the aftermath. I'd love to see it.

80's Miracle Inn disco room!

12

More Star Wars connections, nuclear waste storage, UFO's and top-secret drone testing

There's something going on out there.

Much of what follows can be found out by the reader easily enough online if you do not believe me. As I said before, almost everything within these pages is absolutely true. A source for much of this chapter (someone many locals reading would know) wishes to remain anonymous, and of course I protect my sources. I understand from a purely journalistic standpoint that a reluctance to readily reference facts may seem suspicious. As the reader you will just have to decide for yourself whether this chapter should be taken seriously or not. I urge you to have an open mind.

Pembrokeshire is a mysterious place, but if we want to begin this chapter with a subject and site in Pembrokeshire that could be seen as a centric point for weird, Trecwn could be a good place to start. The village of Trecwn near Haverforwest houses a military/corporate/(former?) Royal Naval arms depot that has secrecy and intrigue surrounding its esoteric legend. The site is known as RNAD Trecwn.

Built as the first bluster of World War Two, it began to inevitably reach even the remotest parts of Europe, it is an even more mysterious site now than it may have seemed straight after its inception. Its early use could be explained as an underground arms depot for munitions for the coming war and later during the Cold War. What is became after, and why it has been purchased over the years by some of the most powerful militarily linked companies in the world, however, is less certain. Some of the strange rumours and stories regarding the site are intriguing. On the less weird but deeply concerning scale of rumour is the belief among many locals that Trecwn is storing nuclear waste material. The site certainly would make sense as a venue for such a thing. Former owners Omega Pacific, an Anglo/Irish company made no secret of their desire to store nuclear material there. They even informed a house of lords select committee of their intentions to do so. Strangely Omega Pacific are also heavily involved in Drone technology and one wonders what else they had in mind at Trecwn. The Manhattan Loft Corporation are the present owners. They too have made no secret of their wish to use the site for esoteric storage use. RNAD Trecwn has 58 massive storage chambers 60 metres in length running into the valley. Some of these tunnels are now bricked up. Many in the area fear that these bricked up tunnels house inimical even highly dangerous material. A Pembrokeshire Herald article from April 2021 quotes concern that Greenpeace have also included Trecwn in a list of sites around the UK that they describe as 'ticking time bombs'. It goes on to report that locals in 2019 were forced to use bottled water as the tap water began to 'look like a tea and smelled strongly of chlorine'! Alarmingly the article ended with this paragraph:

'Water tests carried out at the time in properties on Barham Road showed iron levels of around 1800 micrograms per litre – nine times the legal limit, those properties get their water from a network of pipes that come from RNAD Trecwn and were built when the armament depot was originally constructed.'

The long private road that leads to Trecwn is narrow and silent. Whilst travelling along it toward the mysterious site you can't help but feel the whole area is being watched. There are several you tube videos of civilian drone sorties over Trecwn, but the complex is so large it cannot be covered in one flight. You may think, 'Well, it is so secret how would people be able to fly drones over without being stopped'? Well, because Trecwn's mystery is obviously subterranean. The site itself is so massive and secluded and knowing that most of the working area is underground does make you think. Is there some kind of 'Stranger Things' type plot-line underway behind the steel fencing that rings the entire site?

The weird Pembrokeshire connection to the Star Wars films (see chapter two) is also connected specifically with those valleys. Testing of the 'highball' bouncing bomb with multiple mosquito aircraft attempting to precision bomb the Maenchlochog railway tunnel was carried out here during World War Two. This event was used to form the plot for the 1964 '633 squadron' movie. It is said George Lucas took the bombing scene from 633 to form the story line of the epic precision destruction of the 'Death Star' in the first Star Wars film. Some of the highball bomb casing from the Maenchlochog practice bombing raids is actually on display at Withybush airfield along with a propellor from Lysander aircraft flying from the nearby super-secret wartime Rudbaxton airfield. As an aside, the Lysander was involved in many 'SOE' top secret World War II missions.

Pembrokeshire's connection with 'drone technology' is interesting and, I suspect, not well known by many outside the Ministry of Defence. Military drones have been operated in West Wales for 80 years (the technology is older than you may think). The 'Queen Bee' (hence 'drone') target aircraft was flying from the Manorbier air range from the late 1930s. In more contemporary times the British Army's new surveillance drone is flying from Aberporth and 14 Signal Regiment flies' drones for communication purposes from RAF Brawdy. Castlemartin Range also, has hosted artillery regiments which fly their own drones. The same range in 2013 hosted the US military demonstrating the AH-64E helicopter which flies its own drones. Doubtless MoD Pendine experiments with them also.

RAF Brawdy was also heavily linked with US nuclear submarine technology

and was euphemistically classified as an 'oceanographic research station' in the 1970's. Earlier than that in the 1960's Brawdy was also a 'special' base for the RAF's 'V' squadron of Vulcan bombers that carried the nuclear deterrent. Secret de classified documents show that in the event of a nuclear war the Soviets had lined up THREE one megaton nuclear bombs just for the 'sleepy' village of Brawdy! This illustrates how important that site was in the 20th century's dangerous cold war. In terms of the contemporary nuclear situation, today's main UK nuclear deterrent, the Trident nuclear submarine fleet may well have a future docking home in Milford Haven. Persistent rumours that their current Scottish port Faslane is not a viable base are not going away. The anti-UK union Scottish National Party have in recent years made significant political gains and power in their country - meaning Trident may need a new home soon. Milford Haven's deep waters have been seen by many as a suitable alternative to Faslane. In 2015 a Daily Mail article reported that the then Welsh first minister Carwen Jones welcomed the possible move and the potential employment it would create for Pembrokeshire.

Interestingly, as I write this, a military jet is flying low over my village (Penally) doing some sort of sweeping manoeuvre over and over. Given the history of top-secret military flying craft in Pembrokeshire, so the famous mass 'Welsh Triangle' UFO sightings in Pembs in the 1970's possibly have more earthly connection than many may have thought. At least that is what you MIGHT think, but actually, the head of the RAF police at the time DID conduct an investigation. This was carried out in secret after the year 1977 brought many 'credible' witness reports of Unidentified Flying Objects in the county.

In June 2014 multiple residents of Narberth and Whitland reported seeing a fast-moving 'large star' like object which would occasionally be orbited by smaller 'lights' before drastic course changes seemed to rule out the possibility of satellite activity. Pembrokeshire does seem to have more of this type of sighting than other counties in Wales, often as with the last one I described, involving multiple sighting from Pembrokeshire residents from neighbouring towns and villages. The famous extra-terrestrial mass sighting in Broad Haven in 1977 in which 14 schoolchildren all reported seeing an alien craft and two alien beings, all with more or less the same description was a big story at the time. The off the record account of their schoolmaster, Mrs Morgan, with her assertion that 'I saw it too, you know. It was real!' Is less well known. Mrs Morgan went on to explain to Author Peter Paget that 'When they went, a little whirlwind of dust came across the playground. It was almost as if they were saying goodbye.'

Returning to the Tenby area and the spooky Ridgeway road, many drivers over the years have reported being 'followed' by craft at low altitudes almost always at night. I personally know two people that have claimed the very same thing happened to them whilst driving the road, with a sighting of a low flying triangular glowing object (about 2 or 3 thousand feet), at night, that began to follow them from the outskirts of Pembroke all the way to the edge of Penally before completely disappearing. Not flying away - just disappearing. I mention it because these are friends of mine that do not know each other but have told me the same story. Whether these things are indeed 'alien craft' is an interesting thought but maybe there is something else going on in the skies above us that is equally intriguing. Could it be that Pembrokeshire is a large experimental area for the most modern western military aeronautical technology? Technology that is far ahead in terms of its maneuvering capability than the layman could imagine. Given the county's military, and particularly its drone history dating back to the 1930's, the presumed suitability by the 'powers that be' for Pembrokeshire as being a good testing area for ultra-high-tech military craft seems a real possibility. It is interesting to note that the 'Welsh Triangle' sighting were within the area of latitude 51 degrees 40 minutes North and longitude 5 degrees 8 minutes West. This area incorporating St Brides Bay is riddled with sea caves, some of them with large caverns several hundred yards long. These connect with underground fissures to other caverns and subterranean networks that criss- cross under RAF Brawdy.

13

Magic ancient places, black panthers and Elvis Preseli

This county is old and strange...

Sleepy magic

Ever been somewhere with such an old history that it seems to whisper to your inner thoughts, training your mind that you are in a place alive with the dead? There are several such areas of ancient land in Pembrokeshire that have this ability. The Prehistoric landscape known as Trefloyne between St Florence and Penally is one such a place. Walking along the ancient pathways there that lead to Hoyles Mouth Cave and where the sea once lapped against the ancient banks along what is now a road, can be unnerving but exciting with a little imagination.

It has Celtic royal history that many locals certainly do not realise. There is evidence of a holy site, possibly 5th century named 'Eccluis Guinniau' or the 'Church at Guinniau' around about where Trefloyne golf course is now. The articles and artefacts found at this site over the years suggest an Iron Age Welsh Royal family lived here. Many Welsh saints were said to have been linked to Welsh royal families and this seems true of St Teilo who was probably born at the Church of Guinniau around the year 500. WAY further back than that an even more interesting history concerns Trefloyne. Homosapien stone age people were living in caves in the area, including Hoyles Mouth, since Paleolithic times.

There is evidence that even another species of human -- the Neanderthal -- hunted and raised families here also, in surrounds that probably did not look an awful lot different from how it looks today - about 25,000 years ago. The sociological history of Trefloyne is literally tens of thousands of years old plus, with two species of human possibly sharing some of that time together. As an 11- or 12-year-old I remember heading down there with an old mate also from Penally. We would explore the woods, fields, and the old quarry. Quite bizarrely, so many times we would come across evidence of animal sacrifice! I have a vivid memory of seeing several (possibly) sheep skulls and stones scattered in the shape of pentagrams! Looking back, we would often come across weird black magic ritual evidence! I think it would freak me out more these days than it did then. Clearly though, there is some feeling down that place that attracts those with an interest in esoteric ritual ceremony. When we went that way, we would always bring a torch as inevitably a trip to Hoyles Mouth Cave was on the cards. Entering that cave as an adult as I did recently to research this book, feels just as exciting and strange as it did as a kid. Knowing that people lived in that cave tens of thousands of years ago and sat around telling stories, making tools, creating weaponry, maybe even jewellery, is a trip. I wish I had known back then about the big cat sightings in and around Trefloyne. That would have added spice to those childhood walks. Over the last several decades, there have been multiple sightings of a large black cat like creature in and around the wooded area in that place. I had an unnerving experience a few summers ago whilst cycling along Trefloyne lane on the way to St Florence. As I cycled past the area of the road roughly adjacent to Hoyles Mouth Cave I heard a crash in the trees like something jumping from one tree to the next. As I cycled along, I noticed that whatever it was kept up with me by jumping to the next tree over and over. I could hear leaves rustling and branches snapping, and this continued for about a minute. If it was a squirrel, it was a squirrel on steroids.

A couple of stories coming up from people I know well. They did not wish to give their names, which was disappointing, but I still think it is OK to go ahead and write what they said. So, I will!

As recently as 2016, a local man from Knowling Mead in Tenby was taking a morning walk with his dog (one of those small yappy ones). He often walked up Trefloyne and on to Roberts Wall Farm and then turn back to Tenby. On the day in question, he decided to take that route. When he got about a quarter mile into Trefloyne lane, just near to the golf course entrance, he was stopped in his tracks by what he described as a 'black leopard' crossing the road about 20 yards in front of him. The local man told me, 'It just appeared from the trees and skipped into the hedgerow. It was carrying something, maybe a dead Rat or a Squirrel. After it disappeared my dog wouldn't move and started to whine. I had to pick her up and carry her home! I sort of jogged out of the sheltered Trefloyne lane clutching the dog and was very relieved to get out in the open and onto the main road!' The man further described the sighting to me as, 'Like a big black panther you'd see at the zoo maybe, but a chubby version.'

Another similar sighting, only a year or two before, again made in broad daylight, was made by a business owner friend of mine. He was driving on the Ridgeway road towards Tenby, when, just before the hill into Penally he spotted something moving in the field to the left of the roadside. He told me, 'I saw it straight away. It was really strange, like a black housecat but five times bigger. It was walking with its head bowed down and sort of cantering along close to the hedge but far enough into the field that I could see it. I slowed down to get a good look. I was really close to it, like, meters away. I got my phone out to take a picture and a car came behind me, beeped its horn to get me to move on and the cat thing ran off'. The field he described overlooks Trefloyne. A little research into big cat sightings and it becomes clear that Pembrokeshire has had far more than its fair share. In fact, there have been so many sightings of big cats in Pembrokeshire, that a Gov.com Freedom of information website of exotic cat sightings in Wales clearly shows the county to have had by far the most evidence of this phenomena in terms of sheer reported witness numbers. There have been many of these 'big cat' sightings very recently at Trefloyne, but also in Letterston, Princes Gate, Treffgarne and Jameston. Something to think about!

It is well worth visiting the Tenby museum and seeing the impressive collection of artifacts found at Hoyles Mouth Cave in Trefloyne. The museum also boasts various examples of extinct animal teeth and bones found in the area. These include woolly mammoth tusks, reindeer, and arctic hare bones - meaning stone age Penally dwellers had plenty to hunt. There are also sabre tooth tiger teeth in the museum that were found in Trefloyne. Sabre tooth tigers could stand over a meter tall and two meters in length. They often weighed a quarter of a ton and sported upper canine teeth up to 10 inches long. Suddenly, a black panther sighting or two in the area doesn't seem so bad.

Heading up into the wilds of North Pembrokeshire, the Preseli Hills is another area that radiates a magical and ancient feeling. Everywhere you look around this landscape there are strange stone circles, ancient burial grounds, and hill forts. Heading to a recent solstice up there I was struck by the tangibly weird atmosphere when attending a gathering in the Gwaun Valley. The very light in the Preseli hills is different to anywhere else I have visited in Pembrokeshire. It seems to come partly from the old ground itself and you don't have to be a bit of a hippy or tree hugger to feel that that the land is ancient and very possibly magical. The people up there seem affected by the numinous emanation of the surrounding hills and ancient buried dead. They are, on the whole, a quieter more introspective bunch. To give an example of their anachronistic or possibly mystically insular nature, many in the area, particularly those in the Gwaun Valley, bizarrely, still follow the old Julian Calendar - meaning they celebrate New Year's Day on January 13th!

There are certainly less big cat sightings up there but there is an even weirder claim to fame for the area. It is very possible that Elvis Presley's genealogy comes from within the Preseli hills! Yes, the King! Mr hip-swivelling man himself! Ok... Stay with me... Here we go... So...

The amazing similarity between the names Preseli and Presley must at least make you wonder. Does the recent groundswell of opinion suggesting Elvis' family were in fact from North Pembrokeshire have veridicality? Interestingly an academic from Cardiff university has put forward a compelling case that indeed, the King is from Pembrokeshire. Terry Breverton, a lecturer at the University of Wales points out; Elvis' mother Gladys has a welsh name, his dead twin Jesse Garon Presley had a Welsh second name. Going back further his grandmother Doll Mansell may be of the well-known Mansell family from the Gower Peninsula. There is more. The Bishop of Munster that baptised North Pembrokeshire's St David was Bishop...

You've guessed it... Elvis! There is even a chapel in the Preseli hills dedicated to Saint Elvis – the only one in the country. Nearby there is also as an Elvis close and an Elvis farm. A fair amount of circumstantial evidence wouldn't you say?!

14

The mermaid of Freshwater East

Something from within. To me.

A mysterious tale involving one of the UK's - never mind Pembrokeshire's - most beautiful beaches, namely Freshwater East, does not seem to be well known. For my modest readership I hope at least to let them hear of it. This was purported to have happened or been written, whichever you believe, in the not so distant past.

Peter had been working as a carpenter with a local building firm when he met Beth. She was the daughter of a local landowner that sometimes used Peter's firm for various jobs on his estate near Barafundle Bay in South Pembrokeshire. Beth was beautiful. She had long straight hair, the colour and shine of a raven, with large green eyes the shade of shimmering moss beside a shallow brook. Her face was heart shaped. Under those angelic eyes her nose was diminutive and marble like, her lips always closed with a natural pout and painted crimson, the only make-up she ever wore. The redness of her lips shone against her milk white skin. Her perfume was from the soap she used only. It was a special variety gifted to her often from family in Paris. It could affect like early jasmine on a breeze. She always wore long flowing red or white dresses that draped along the ground as she walked so it looked like she was gliding and not walking. The dresses she made herself, always had a sash across her tiny waistline. One of red if she wore a white dress, or white if she wore a red dress. Beth was disliked by some in the villages that bordered her father's land. Her esoteric wistful manner and the unusual way she dressed made her quite different from local girls from land owning families that could have become friends. Some found her intimidating. Her intense beauty made sure that she was actively disliked by others. Men would pass her in the village and had no courage to speak with her, always unsure how to even try. They saw her, maybe, as like a grace beyond them. She was not allowed to work as her strict father thought it beneath her but was encouraged to read at the family library and learn the ways of the world within books. Her father hoped that at some point she would notice one of the young, landed men that would accompany their rich families when visiting their estate. They of course, always fell for her.

Peter was older than Beth, being into his thirty sixth year. Beth was not yet 22. Peter was a weather beaten but handsome man. His blue eyes, steely tanned face and sandy hair meant that his Pembrokeshire linage was probably Norse, like many in the county. Peter was fit and strong and worked long hours. He was wiry, stood straight and always dressed without pretention. There was an anger within him or maybe a sadness for something he lost a long time ago. In the evenings Peter did not join the others he worked with at the tavern very often although he did occasionally go there. Others found him a tad aloof, but he was not disliked as such. Peter found other people difficult. Whether it be with a girl he met that he began something with, or friendships that were not cultivated. His sadness was often surface deep. In the evenings after work, mostly he would sit in his home on the cliffs above Freshwater East beach, a simple wooden dwelling that he had built in that remote spot himself. He would read something untaxing and drink bramble wine. Then he would take his bottle and walk down the steep cliff path and into the shallows of Freshwater East's sea for hours at a time.

He would look at the rocks of the cliffs that framed the inshore sea. He would imagine from time to time that he would see a naked beautiful girl with cascading blond curls watching him from the sea as the wine washed away the day's earlier reality. She had the darkest, almost black flashing eyes, and Peter would see her through the sea mist as the wine and the magical place itself filled his head with tranquil night-time light. Sometimes he would sleep on the beach and would dream of his vision. As he slept, he would become lost within her spell and they would become as one. Then it was as if he felt the slight weight of her ghostly white face and golden hair resting upon his chest as he slept. He would often wake at dawn with a bittersweet longing. So, this was his lot, and along with it he worked hard during the day. He drank wine at night too often now as he was surely missing something he needed. He was tough and strong and did not ever consciously think of himself as suffering. But, despite his pertinacity, he was lonely. Beth was also lonely, but unlike Peter, she smiled at people she met and hoped for the future.

One summer they would meet. Peter had been repairing a fence line more than a mile in length that cut across a steep turning field overlooking Barafundle Bay. Beth liked to walk this land and watch the gypsy shire horses grazing, with the expansive green sea in the distance. This July afternoon Beth was walking this stretch in glorious warm sunshine, occasionally stooping to pick wildflowers. After a time, she had a perfect bunch of white daisies, peppered with blue grape hyacinth and pink flecks from the occasional rose campion. Peter had his head down working away and shoring up a damaged piece of fence line. Beth in her shimmering white summer dress and red sash swaying as she stepped left a sheltered turn and came upon Peter suddenly. She stopped in her tracks on the sloping ground almost upon him. Peter looked up. He made out her slender figure only as a shimmering silhouette for a moment as the sun behind Beth poured into his eyes. He stood up and saw her this time completely. His knees became weak, and he actually had to steady himself against the wooden fencing, feeling as though on a carriage that had stopped suddenly. It was as if he had come to the end of a long journey the moment he looked upon her for the first time. Beth for her part stood still looking only at Peter, hands together but arms down, unaware that the flowers she held were cascading one by one onto the ground.

'Oh, you have dropped your flowers.' said Peter and stooped to begin gathering them. He stood and handed Beth the dozen or so daisies.

She nodded thanks, not looking into his eyes. She suddenly, almost involuntarily asked, 'What is your name sir?' and held the flowers against her chest.

'I am Peter,' he answered. 'Oh look, there is a feather, just here.' Peter with his forefinger gently brushed Beth's ink black hair above her left eye behind her ear and let the feather drift into the slight warm breeze that led out to sea. Beth did not flinch or protest as Peter did this but closed her eyes in gratitude for his gentle touch and the connection of love that was filling her body as they stood so close.

'Thank you, Sir. oh, I mean, Peter. Or should I call you sir?!' stammered Beth.

'Please call me Peter.'

There was a silence as they looked at each other. Peter was lost in Beth's eyes that were the colour in the sun of the shallow warm emerald waters of Barafundle Bay below them. Beth looked into Peter's warm blue eyes, embarrassed to do so quite so obviously, but was drawn to see him, as he was with her.

'What do they call you miss?' asked Peter in a suddenly weakened voice that surprised him a little. He looked at her hands holding the flowers, and though she wore rings, there were none that encircled another's heart. Beth saw him look to her hands, understood and blushed.

'If you are not in a hurry miss, um, Beth. Would you like to take tea with me here? I was just about to put the pot on the fire.'

'Yes, please Peter.' Beth returned, even before Peter had finished his last syllable.

'We are alone up here Beth. Is that OK? Though I don't suppose two people having tea should offend anyone.' Peter smiled as he said this. Beth was not in the slightest bit worried about how anything seemed regarding etiquette that afternoon. Soon they were sat on a patch of flat grass with Beth's wooden cup of almost untouched tea (Peter only had one vessel with him). Her flowers she had tied in grass. They looked upon one another. They were mentioning the colours of nature around them, the white of the sea foam and how grand was the heaving blue cloudless sky above. In reality, they were only looking upon one another, and both falling in love. They sat and barely spoke. After only a full minute or so, Peter took Beth's hands with his. She did not flinch but let him take them up. He lowered his head and kissed the back of her right hand. In the next moment they were embraced as lovers and Peter kissed her deeply with both completely lost in the other. Soon Beth felt the warmth of the sun on her naked body and Peter knew that she was his and that now he belonged to her. They made love passionately but gently out there in the open with only the sound of their fevered breathing and the lapping of the Sea on the beach in the bay, way below them.

Afterwards, they dressed quickly, realising finally that somebody could come upon them at any time. Still, they lay there together, heads propped by their hands. From where they were, they could see if someone were coming upon them from a distance if they paid mind. They spoke into each other's eyes. Peter learned who she was, and she him. Peter knew that Beth's father would never permit them to be together. Beth protested that she would never be apart from Peter and Peter knew that he could never be apart from her. That very hour they planned to meet at Peter's house in Freshwater East the next day, which was a Saturday, and they would look at what they could do. They had both realised their lives would change from here on in and it did not matter what were the consequences for either, as long as they were together. As the weeks went by, they met as often as was safe without anyone in the village's knowledge and their love became more important than the world.

In the weeks following that first meeting they had spent most of their time when together at Peter's wooden dwelling. It was built into the cliffs of Freshwater East away from prying eyes. Their time together was always short as the walk from Freshwater to Barafundle was long. Though her father knew Beth enjoyed long walks and permitted this, Beth could not explain an extended absence, even on a Saturday, traditionally her day, and so the day of the week Peter and Beth had always met at his home. Tonight was Saturday and they would make a plan to be together forever that evening, no matter what, even if it meant them running away and starting a new life. Peter sat in his home and thought about the possible future while waiting for Beth. He took a glass of wine and tasted it. He realised he had not drunk from his barrel of bramble wine since meeting Beth some two months earlier and was surprised at how he felt the strength of the first glass. He heard a distant call from the shore below that was full of longing and he took another sip of wine. Enjoying the sweetness of the blood red blackberry flavour and letting his mind drift as he looked down at the beach, it suddenly came to him. He had not yet walked with Beth on the beautiful shoreline below. He resolved they would go there that evening. Peter made it as a toast to himself and downed his glass, then poured another. Beth soon arrived dressed in a beautiful white satin dress with a silk sash of red across her waist that matched her blood red lips. Peter took her in his arms and kissed Beth with passion and they both fell backwards onto the wooden floor. Beth was for once a little taken aback. She held his shoulders at arm's length as they drew apart on the ground and looked at him a little differently than she had before.

'Is that wine I taste? Your lips are as red as mine.' She smiled.

'I'm sorry. I lost my balance a little there. Are you ok?' He held her hand and lifted her to standing.

'I'm fine.' She smiled and felt his concerning love with the question. They retired to where Peter slept and made love with the sound of the gulls above and the gentle swooshing of the waves below drifting through the window. After this they lay on the bedclothes, naked together, and looked into each other's eyes. Peter surveyed her porcelain like perfect female frame and brushed her hair behind her ears just as he had the first time they met.

'Can we walk on the shore below tonight?' Peter asked.

'Of course,' said Beth. 'I have wanted to since I first came here. It is one of the beaches in Ros to which I have not been. Though I feel I know it, I have seen it from your window so many times. I do not have long, however. We haven't discussed...'

'Yes, of course.' Peter interrupted uncharacteristically curtly.

Beth, surprised at his slightly brusque response returned, 'We can discuss it as we walk.'

Peter rose from the bed and began to dress. Suddenly finding himself, he answered more gently this time. 'That would be good. I do not ever want to be without you my darling. The nights here are lonely now; and our meetings on the estate, which are so dangerous for our love, are not for the future. Every time you come here too, you risk being seen and having your reputation ruined in this part of the world. It may be that we have to find another land to start again.'

'Whatever it may take,' whispered Beth.

'My nights without you... Dreaming of you is not enough!' Peter continued as he picked up his wine from the table. He swallowed what was left in the glass and held the empty vessel with his head bowed. Then, suddenly, Peter looked to the window and the sea below. He was in deep thought and concentrating, as though he were listening intently at someone calling for him from a distance. Peter's arms were draped straight down with both hands holding the empty glass by their fingertips. Suddenly it slipped from his fingers and dropped to the floor, just as the wildflowers did from Beth the first day they met. The glass did not break, and Beth stepped off the bed to pick it up, but Peter took it back from her and walked to the kitchen placing it on top of the Bramble barrel. Beth dressed quickly looking to the kitchen and wondering things she had not thought before. Mainly though, she thought with concern.

It was a very quiet spot up there on the cliffs above Freshwater East beach. They were still cautious but felt confident to walk down together and probably would not be seen. Certainly not by anyone that knew Beth. The first time they were spotted together they could say Peter worked for her father and that they had met by chance. They did not wish to give up this advantage too early, however.

'Shall we go?' asked Beth. 'I can leave from the beach after we talk.'

'I will, as always, then follow you home from a distance,' answered Peter. 'Here, let us take this'. Peter picked up the bottle of bramble wine from atop the barrel and Beth looked down at the ground as Peter took her hand. They walked outside onto the steep secluded cliff path. A gentle calling in the distance turned out to be the breeze whistling on the opened wine bottle. Peter held Beth's hand and they walked onto the beach noting that they seemed to be alone. Peter took a drink straight from the bramble wine bottle and Beth looked a little annoyed with Peter for the first time. 'Can you take the wine at less frequent intervals?' she implored.

'You have never seen me drink dearest,' said Peter. 'Don't worry, it is still me and I have not become another.'

'I just think as we are to talk, Peter. About what we should do next. I love you and I know you love me. Let us plan our strategy. Can you leave this county with me?'

As Beth asked this question Peter took a long drink from his wine and a distant female voice was plainly drifting to Peter and Beth from out to sea! It was singing, in a mournful but almost angry tone.

> *'She may be a beauty with no rival upon land*
> *She may have won his heart when she first took his hand But I*
> *am in the wine and I sing from the Sea*
> *I wish to take his soul -- only HE can stop me'*

'Is someone in peril, Peter? What IS that sound? It makes me afraid...' The singing continued.

> *'So I warm his very chest with my powerful breath And yet I*
> *bring him love I can also bring him death She must be very still*
> *and sadly watch me play*
> *If he will not resist me, then her love will end today'*

Beth watched in complete stupefaction as she saw the mermaid gliding through the water towards them. A calm sea rippled around her as her smiling face, as hypnotising and beautiful as Beth had ever seen, became clear to the couple on land. Beth realised it was this 'woman' that had been singing to them. The mermaid, like a cobra would for a snake charmer, swayed upright, from side to side in the water. Her beautiful golden hair clinging with the water to her naked breasts. She was perfect to behold. Her eyes were flashing black and gold as she swayed from side to side. Beth looked on and saw the mermaid's perfect torso and wild hair cascading down to her midriff which was decorated with a ruby on her navel. The tail swimming elegantly letting her 'hover' in the water. She began once more to sing, but just to Peter (he had drifted away from Beth and was up to his ankles in the water still holding the bottle) and the beautiful mermaid held her hand up at Beth as if to command her to be still:

> 'Human Change me to your form, together let us be, Let your senses harden but your mind become unfree.
> Take me here and take me now, yes you should have your fun.
> That love you had when it is over, Beth will make it done'

The sea creature stepped from the sea as a perfect human form. The most sensual and slender body stepped directly into Peter as they fell to the sand together. The embrace became a desperate show for Beth who found herself powerless to stop this from happening or even to move, or even to look away! Peter and the mermaid engaged in a very different form of love to that which Beth had known with Peter. It was animal and without goodness. Beth found herself lightheaded and finally passed out there on the sand.

Sometime later she came to as the sea lapped around her feet, the night drawing in. She sat up and looked to where the terrible scene had been before. Peter slept there, snoring loudly, the now empty bottle still within his hand. Beth stood up with anger and felt her strength with the anger. Sadness would be for another time. She walked off Freshwater East Beach and left her love for Peter behind.

Freshwater East Beach

15

Pembrokeshire and the otherworld: witches, wizards, and magic

Magic, allegories and Megan the witch

Mermaids in Freshwater East are one thing, but Pembrokeshire has a rich history involving the mystic and supernatural in general. The concentration of people with 'special' gifts is thicker in Pembrokeshire than most other counties in Britain. The 'Mabinogion' folk tales are mainly set in Western Wales and their Celtic supernatural legend still lives on. It is also said that the Flemings that came here in the 12th century were naturally gifted with strange powers that included divination and were known for reading the bones of animals to tell fortunes and heed warnings etc. Many of their descendants are of course still here. There are many tales in Pembrokeshire of Wizards or 'knowing men' and most villages and towns in the county have at least one famous wizard that would practice there generations earlier. Witches too are prominently featured in Pembrokeshire's folk History. Brian John's excellent and charming 2001 tome 'Pembrokeshire Wizards and Witches' lists many stories involving their sometimes benevolent, sometimes malevolent actions. During the eighteenth Century, as well as Wizards, there were also witches known to be in all of the towns and most of the villages in Pembrokeshire. John's book mentions by name many of these characters.

Old Moll of Redberth, Dolly Llewellin of Carew Newton and Molly Newton of Pembroke Dock stick out for me. Pembroke Dock is still full of witches and even has contemporary Wizards that have been known to make household electrical goods, jewellery, wallets and even cars disappear.

Wales as a whole has a very tolerant historical line when it comes to the practice of magic. In the insane period of mass hysteria which covered the Witch burnings of the early modern era it is notable that in Wales prosecution of 'witches' was very rare indeed. Officially, five were executed in Wales during that sad period of history. To put that into perspective, the numbers in Scotland and England were possibly many thousands, though no absolutely reliable figures are available. Different sources both official and in many contemporary and historical books of the period quote wildly differing numbers, but they were significant. While Scotland and England went with the European 'Christian' witch purge the Welsh were far more tolerant of 'knowing' people. Outside Britain, again an exact figure is unknown, but possibly 200,000 plus women were murdered by the state across Europe and in parts of North America during this awful period. Wales can be genuinely proud not to have joined in with the insanity, at least not on a mass scale. There was always a comfortable co-existence of the natural and supernatural in Wales that may well have had much to do with the Celtic language and roots. In Pembrokeshire there were no executions of witches and only a few cases mentioned when the law got involved with alleged witchcraft.

As an oddity however, Pembrokeshire does lay claim to the earliest reference to witchcraft in Wales. At the beginning of the 16th century (1502 or 1503) John Morgan, the Bishop of St David no less, claimed he had had two assassination attempts on him by consecutive witches. Bishop Morgan had intervened in a case of adultery among some members of his parish and became targeted by the cheating couple involved. They allegedly hired consecutive witches from Bristol to 'destroy' the Bishop. Interestingly Pembrokeshire also can claim the last inditement for the 'crime' of witchcraft. As late as 1699 Haverfordwest Castle was used as the venue to hear the case against a Dorcas Heddin. She was accused of cursing a ship and bewitching sailors on the way to Virginia. Dorcas claimed that the Devil appeared to her as 'a black man' and demanded three drops of her blood to do her bidding. Dorcas claims that rather than curse the ship and put the whole crew in danger, she only wished to target two men that had 'short rationed' her earlier. The surnames of some of these Pembrokeshire accused witches are familiar still in the towns and villages today. Take Katherine Lewis, wife of a Thomas Bowen of Tenby (1607), Olly Powell of Loverston (1693), or male witch Tom Eynon of Lamphey (1840).

Wizards too play a prominent role in the mystical history of Pembrokeshire. Merlin the magician (possibly 6th century) may have been a real person that was known for having the gift of 'knowing'. Although he was reputed to have been from Carmarthenshire originally, he is said to have had many links to Pembrokeshire. Some of the place names (Merlin's Bridge and Merlin's Hill) in Haverfordwest allude to his links to the county and he was said to have made his home in Manorbier for a time. Prince Pwyll of the Mabinogion stories and his links to the allegedly still bewitched Narberth Castle mound are fun to read and find out about. Pembrokeshire has many stories about men such as John Harries, Abe Biddle and Wil Tiriet that were purported to have been able to see into the future and perform many miraculous deeds. Unlike many witches, wizards were mainly understood to have had benevolent intentions. Although many men were executed as witches during the witch trials era, it is notable that more than 80% of the victims of the 'holy' purge were women.

As an odd addendum for my writing on witch trial era it is interesting to note that Shakespeare's Macbeth, written in the middle of this time and featuring a coven of witches as well as all kinds of black magic, has a Pembrokeshire connection. The 'thanes of Cawdor' in that work were based on a real family, the descendants of which are the Cawdors of Stackpole. They lived in Pembrokeshire for 260 years, right up into the 1960's. Earl Cawdor, of Castlemartin is still a Peerage title in the UK.

In the 21st century Pembrokeshire still boasts a relatively large population of faith healers and 'white' witches. The use of 'charms' is widespread in this part of the country too, with horseshoe doorknockers still often seen on cottages and houses in the villages. Horseshoe doorknockers are known to ward off evil spirits. Also, many people in Pembrokeshire have a basic understanding of herbal medicine and harmless superstitions are more prevalent here than in other parts of the UK. The mystical and ancient sociological Pembrokeshire links are certain to play a part in the Pembrovian's mind being more open to the possibility of the existence of the 'other' supernatural world.

A story about a witch called Megan from my home village of Penally is not well known in Pembrokeshire. I think it should be...

Megan of Middlewalls Lane

There once was a rich old man in Penally that only thought about times gone by. His wife had passed on many years before. He had been a very good-looking youth and had stayed a handsome man well into his 60's, but that was a long time ago.

David, as was his name, was sitting in his front room with a fire going on the eve of his 90th birthday. The date being October the 30th, 1850. David stoked his fire and saw that it burned well. As always on the eve of his birthday he took a good bottle of
whiskey from his stores and wore fine clothes. His face was lined but with a grace and sharp featured. He was tall and slender and though his hair was almost white it was still thick and looked well upon his head. David moaned about being old and did not appreciate his luck in reaching advanced age. However, he still wished to go on and enjoy the goods his past had provided for him in his old age. He had been a successful lime pit owner many years before but had no children to pass on his success and had sold the business long ago for a small fortune. Many people in the county knew of his riches and wondered, when the time came, who would receive his bequeathment.

David was not penurious but was also not a spendthrift. He had one mirror in his house in that front room, just a small oval shaped piece of glass that sat next to the clock on the mantelpiece. On certain dates, after some considerable amount of whiskey he would look into that mirror, talk to himself and his tired old face, lament on how things once were, and on how little time he had left. On that evening he noticed the time by the clock on the mantlepiece that it was just about to strike midnight. He took his whiskey bottle and topped up his glass. He took a sip, and then a gulp, shivered all over with leathery sweet warmth and saw that by the clock hands it was now his birthday, as well as the mystical date of Halloween. He said happy birthday to himself, put down his glass and walked over to the mirror. 'What would I not give to lose 30… neigh… 20 years! I was so nimble at 70!'. Oh. But better! To be 60 again!!! To see my wonderful wife. She went before I was 65 years old. She was not yet 45. Alas. I am 90! Where to go from here!?' His pitch rose with these last few words and at the end of them David took another gulp of warming whiskey. He was comfortably drunk and stared into the fire with its hypnotic glow. He fancied within the twisting flames that a hare was bounding along the strange dimensions of the numinous lights. Suddenly, there was a knock on the door!

Three taps in quick succession. This was an unusual occurrence. David had visitors from time to time but never at this hour. David put down his glass and walked to the kitchen, picked up a small cudgel he kept behind the door there and then walked to the front door.

'Who's there?' He spoke sharply.

There was no reply, only the sound of the rain. 'Who's there?!' He spouted more gruffly. After a few more seconds there finally came a reply.

'It is I, Megan.' croaked an old lady's voice.

'Megan?!' said David, now more confused than concerned. 'Please, let an old woman into your house. I am caught in this howling weather.'

Aside his vanity and his present drunkenness, David was a decent enough old man. One by one he pulled open the three bolts that secured his heavy old oak door and heaved it open. There stood Megan dripping wet in her long black shawl, face half covered with its sopping hood that draped over her eyes and hung to her nose.

'Come in.' said David. His late guest stepped into his house. David closed the door behind her and bade her come into the front room and sit by the fire.

'There was once a person very important to me named Megan.' said David, in a matter-of-fact way. He watched her walk ahead and surveyed her tiny frame within the thin soaked shawl. She carried a walking stick, hobbled into the fire lit room, choose David's favourite seat, then turned around and sank back into it. She then pulled her hood from over her head. She had long straight silver-grey hair, it was the colour of a spider's web caught in the fire light. She looked about her and saw shelves lined with leather bound books, thick drapes over the window, various framed pictures of vaguely familiar royalty and a wooden floor with a great

Axminster rug covering much of the living area. It was cosy and warm, slightly stale and very comfortable. Megan looked up at David as he stepped across the room and

stood next to the fireplace looking down upon her, his elbow resting on the mantel shelf next to the mirror. He looked into her face and saw that it seemed a little younger than his but still aged. Her eyes were light blue and sharp. Like him, her nose was thin and etched finely into her features. Her lips were tight and closed. She looked into David's eyes and they surveyed each other with only the sound of the crackling fire and the rain tapping on the window.

'I have seen you from time-to-time, just lately, walking from Penally toward Tenby and then back again,' said David.

'Aye.' said Megan. There followed another silence.

'Can I offer you something to drink? I can put the kettle on the fire and make tea or...'

'I see you have whiskey from the north,' interrupted Megan. 'May I have some to warm these old bones?'

'Well, yes of course.' answered David. He took a new glass from his drinks cabinet and picked up the bottle that he had half emptied himself that very evening. He handed Megan the glass and bent to pour her a drink. Megan snatched the bottle from David and suddenly filled her glass to the brim then held the almost empty bottle out for David to take back. He took it with surprise and stood over Megan. Megan held her glass in front of her, it was so full she spilt a drop or two onto the floor.

'For the fairies!' Megan croaked. She then looked up at David standing over her and began to empty the glass into her mouth. In three slow gulps and looking straight into his eyes the old woman drained the vessel.

'Ahhh' said Megan with a satisfied air.

'Goodness me!' spouted David.

'Ha ha ha ha ha! It is good.' said Megan and her lips smacked together. David saw she had but several teeth in her old head. She continued to look up into David's surprised old face. 'I hope you are knowing spirits!' David said aghast. That was quite a...'

'Yes, I am knowing spirits, David Powell! As I know you.'

'Many know me,' said David. He then sat on the only other seat, a wooden chair next to the fire and poured the rest of the bottle into his glass. He took a sip and looked upon the old woman lit by the flashing fire. Shadows danced about her. She was like a crouched old housecat in the flickering light. David again investigated her face and saw that it was lined and pale. Her eyes though, like those of a young blue-eyed raven, looked upon him and he thought he knew them from some time before.

'You wish you were a young man again, David. Why can you not look back upon your life and feel at one with the blessing of old age?' David sat in confusion. He looked upon Megan smiling back at him and angrily said 'What do you know of my thoughts? I am happy to be old and do not think of such foolish things.'

'When you lie to me David Powell, I see a horned demon dancing upon your tongue!' Megan answered. 'Tell me David, what would you give to take back the years!? Imagine it! As you have so many times before?' Megan said these words and then strangely smiled. Her eyes, David thought, gave a flash in the firelight.

'I am a poor old woman and wish for security. I do not want to live door to door on the charitable whim of a stranger anymore. You are rich, and like I, alone. We could be happy here with each other's company in this grand old cottage on Middlewalls lane. Take another bottle from your store and pour us another drink, I will show you something dark and mystical. Something you want.'

David stood up and said, 'What have we here for a birthday! A poor old beggar comes to MY cottage and says she will grant me what I WANT at midnight, in the midst of a storm! Why, this is as an old tale. But then I am an old man. Though you

see I can move as someone younger. Yes. I shall fetch another bottle old woman. Then you shall not think to disappoint me.'

The night rained on outside, the wind howled away, but inside the snug cottage the fire crackled and fed the room with a comfortable warmth.

David quickly returned with another bottle.

'Pass me that, old man.' snapped Megan.

'Here!' said David sharply. 'Do another as you just did. We will see what you know.' He handed the old woman the bottle.

'Take that mirror from above the fire and draw your chair next to mine.' commanded Megan. She took David's now almost empty glass and placed it next to her own on the old wooden floor in front of them. She took the whiskey bottle and half-filled each glass, then stood up and reached into a pouch in her garment producing a handful of honeysuckle.

'These are young colours from the Holloway nearby. Let them fall as they will and produce an elixir for two.' Megan sprinkled the flowers above the glasses with many dropping into the spirits below. She closed her eyes and uttered her next words softly as if in prayer.

'Take the mirror in your left hand. Watch me take this the glass of spirit in my right.'

'Hold the mirror in front of me. Now watch it as I drink'. Megan took a sip, then another. David looked within the mirror as he was told. He watched the image of Megan drinking the whiskey and flowers and wondered what the game was all about. He suddenly became aware that the sound of rain on the window had ceased and the wind had lulled. The room was silent, aside the lowing crackling of the fire. He watched the mirror and saw Megan drink from the glass. Something was not as normal here. With each sip the old woman became less old! With each gulp, so her

skin tightened. Her hair became less grey and more coloured, until, before David knew it, as chestnut brown! Another gulp, then another.

The glass was now drained. David looked into the mirror, now shaking in his left hand and saw the face of his wife as a young woman. Her face heart shaped, lips full. Her dark blue eyes large and decorated with long black lashes. Her cheeks rosy and ripe. Perhaps 23 or so. The age she was when she married him.

David, shaking, managed to place the mirror on the ground and, looking into the glowing fire, asked, 'Do I dare look at you outside the mirror?'

Megan's voice, now youthful and clear like a softly ringing bell, almost timidly spoke back, 'Do not look at me again until you have picked up the mirror and drained your glass also. Watch yourself as you do this. You will look upon yourself and see 50 years disappear. You will become young once again!'

David picked up the mirror and again held it in his left hand. He looked at his image in the mirror, and, still shaking, watched himself drink down his glass, honeysuckle and all. He saw as his face become as suddenly from old to mere middle age. He stared into the mirror looking back at a man half a century younger than the one that had begun the evening. His hair had become black and his features shone with life and were handsome once again. His body felt strong despite his shock.

'Now you may look upon me once more David.' Megan spoke with a soft feminine utterance. David did look, and saw his young wife smiling back at him. 'We will go to our bedchamber now and hold each other. You will wake on the morrow and remember not this night, but just our life as it is. People will see us as they always did. I will be comfortable here.'

'As will I!' exclaimed David.

'You will not have learned much,' spoke his beautiful young wife, 'But here I am.

And here I will stay.' Megan led him to bed. She undressed from her shawl to reveal her youthful nakedness. They passed the next hour lovingly together, before finally sleeping, as do the dead. In the morning Megan brought tea to David and softly woke him.

'Happy Birthday, my love.' she whispered.

David sleepily looked into her eyes. He sat up suddenly. 'Oh yes! And what a birthday is this! How dreadful to be 40!' he said with disgust, 'Yes, you are young, and I am glad you are my wife. But I am middle aged. My best days are behind me. How sad to be so old. What would I give to be as a mere youth once more?!'

16

Pembrokeshire forever -- Let us drift with the tides

... and ever

I am not sure if Pembrokeshire people that have moved away have pictures of their home county on the wall (I didn't), but it is interesting to note that every family in Pembrokeshire seems to have at least one picture or painting somewhere in their home, of Tenby Harbour. I have even been to a friend's place in Tenby that overlooked Tenby harbour, and they had a picture of the harbour next to the window that framed the actual view of Tenby harbour. For me as a Tenby boy, that image of the harbour, done to death in watercolour, sketch or picture is sort of seared into my DNA. It is certainly not an unpleasant image, but it is amazing how that picture has become ubiquitous in this western place. Without careful checks, its familiarity can provoke a listless feel without appreciating the fortunate nature of having come from within such a homeland. In this world that contains everything good and bad, it could have been so much worse. In fact, for the Pembrokeshire ilk, it could hardly have been much better.

The people of Pembrokeshire go away but always come back. To settle outside is always to suffer the very distant, almost faint, but very definite peel of bells from the old parish. They could be those of Penally, Bosherston, St Davids, Pembroke or maybe Lamphey. But all the same, there it is. A sentimental tinnitus.

The change in the world over the last century has perhaps been more concentrated and quickly marked than in any other era. It is fascinating for me to note the changes during my Grandfather Harold Phillips' life. He was born in a house on Tenby harbour in 1911 and left this earth in 2007. In his 96 years a few things happened historically. For his first decades in Tenby when he lived with his family in what is now the Caldey shop, there were few telephones in houses, the modern computer was far from being conceived and it was 'Shank's Pony' or the horse and Cart that was the main mode of transport for short journeys. By his final decades there were satellites orbiting the earth, smartphone technology and the internet. Despite worldly changes, one suspects that Tenby to my grandfather seemed unchanging. A constant gift from a county that's architecture is dominated by a natural and ancient aspect. Pembrokeshire does of course incorporate the modern world in many ways, but the modern world is yet to fully incorporate Pembrokeshire. It still does feel, being down here, that you are, as such, tucked away from the rat race. It is similar in some ways in other rural counties in the UK, but Pembrokeshire is more cut off than most thanks to infrastructural and literal geographic matters. There is no motorway for an hour's drive if you live in the western part of Pembs and the one horse trainline option to Swansea, for changes to London and other cities can be laughably slow and cumbersome.

Pembrokeshire can be an inconvenient place in terms of many things. Its literal position is inconvenient. Its lack of choice for a steady professional career is inconvenient. Its distance from an airport is really inconvenient. Right now, at my time of writing, in Tenby there is a quarter ton Walrus on the new lifeboat slip that is inconvenient. Convenience, however, is not always to a person's long-term advantage. For many young people in the county, it is the thought of leaving and broadening the horizons that appeals.

I was certainly one of those people not long ago. But whether I live in my home county or far from it, these days I understand and appreciate it more. It is a great idea to leave anywhere you started in life when the time comes and to examine the world. Also, in terms of Pembrokeshire, living away from it for a time really does help a person understand that indeed, they are lucky to be from such a place. To know Pembrokeshire's old landscape is always lying somewhere over there in the West - taking it easy for the sinners of the world, in the warm Tenby sun or cooling in the misty Hills of Preseli, while you may be in some stuffy office in London or working in some unfamiliar foreign land -- is a comfort. It is easy to be snobbish about that place way out in the west. It is easy, when in some modern city somewhere, to think of Pembrokeshire and feel as though there is no hand to progression within that place. Certainly, in terms that it does not obviously contain any such cultural or sophisticated vanguard of any kind. But what is progression anyway? Is it not a subjective abstraction?

It is possible that many of the people of Pembrokeshire drift along as the clouds do above. The older families here bequeathing the place with a certain type that has not disappeared yet. Citing once more the great Edward Laws -- so in Pembrokeshire all is a little disordered here and there. Speaking in the late Victorian era he states that in fact, in that western place, 'love children' abound, and a girl who has tripped is not considered to have erred very grievously. This tolerance seems to be of Kymric origin. Unlike the Welshmen our Little Englanders are good horsemen and bold sailors, qualities inherited from their Norse ancestors; heavy drinkers too, a failing we may perhaps attribute to the same source. They are, however, not quarrelsome when in their cups.

That seems a fair enough summing up of it to me! A laid-back land with a laid-back people. A people also with a historical acceptance of the mystic and traditional, of magic and superstition. A knowing set in many ways. They inhabit a quite different place to other welsh counties. A historical anomaly that perhaps is not entirely certain of its allegiance within its own Principality. It is not entirely Welsh, certainly not entirely English, but maybe more British than anything. Perhaps one of the only counties in the United Kingdom that feels it does not first of all belong to one of the home nations, but of the collective.

Pembrokeshire does not need to, nor wish to give up its past as many places seem to will. Also, that county is still not tainted enough by the busted hum of the modern world for anyone to get too cynical about its contemporary drawbacks. In fact, because of Pembrokeshire's timeless aspect and its disavowing nature regarding any particular extreme, so it will continue going nowhere at a pretty and pleasant pace.

* * *

Selected Bibliography

Books

Harry (2020) St Nicolas & St Tielo Church, Penally: It's History from Celtic Times to the Present Day. Tenby: Tredeml Print.

John, B. S. (1979) The Geology of Pembrokeshire. Cardigan: Abercastle Publications.

John, B. S. (2001) Pembrokeshire Wizards and Witches. Newport: Greencroft Books.

Paget, P. (2018) The Welsh Triangle Revisited. St Albans: Panther Grenada. Winn, C. (2007) I Never Knew that about Wales. London: Penguin.

Willison, C. (2013) Pembrokeshire Folk Tales. Stroud: The History Press.

Journal

Allen, W. O. B. (1885) The Flemings and their Chimneys in Pembrokeshire, Journal of the British Archaeological Association, 41(2), p. 117-123.

Blogs

Chandler, A. "RNAD Trecwn Could be 'Ticking Time Bomb' Says Greenpeace". http://pembrokeshire-herald.com/64896/rnad-trecwn-could-be-ticking-time-bomb-says-greenpeace/.

Deacon, T. "The history of witchcraft in Wales". https://www.walesonline.co.uk/news/wales-news/history-witchcraft-wales-15334964.

Eberlin, A. "The Flemings of Pembrokeshire". https://flemish.wp.st-andrews.ac.uk/2015/0/02/the-flemings-of-pembrokeshire/.

Gitlin, J. "Dating Apps Are Common, Useful—and Widely Disliked." https://www.surveymonkey.co.uk/curiosity/dating-apps-and-sites-are-almost-as-common-as-they-are-disliked/.

Sinclair,T. "Grants Tender Process 'Corrupt'". http://pembrokeshire-herald.com/3506/grants-tender-process-corrupt-2/.

William, J. "A Recipe for Corruption". https://jacobwilliams.com/8790/a-recipe-for-corruption/.

William, J. "Running Gag". https://jacobwilliams.com/14461/running-gag/.

Websites

BBC News. "Elvis the King of Cymru". http://news.bbc.co.uk/2/hi/uk_news/wale/774228.stm#:~:text=The%20king%20of%20rock%20and,Preseli%20hills%20in%2 west%20Wales.&text=%22His%20dead%20twi%2C%20Jesse%20Garon,too%2C%2%20said%20Mr%20Breverton.

BBC News. "Millennium Falcon was Pembroke Dock's 'Best Kept Secret'". https://www.bbc.com/news/av/uk-wales-38039483.

Tenby Today. "County Council under Fire from One of Its Own". https://www.tenby-today.co.uk/article.cfm?id=929headline=County%20Council%20under%20fire%20from%20one%20of%20its%20own&sectionIs=news&search year=2014.

Welsh Government. "Big Cat Sightings". https://gov.wales/atisn14172. Western Telegraph. "Pembroke Dock's Defensible Barracks up for Sale". https://www.westerntelegraph.co.uk/news/17362222.pembroke-docks-defensible-barracks-sale/.

Western Telegraph. "Declassified Documents Reveal How RAF Brawdy Was a Target for Soviet Union Nuclear Missiles". https://www.westerntelegraph.co.uk/news/11269697.declassified-documents-reveal-how-raf-brawdy-was-a-target-for-soviet-union-nuclear-missiles/.

Western Telegraph. "Half of All Welsh Big Cat Sightings Are in Pem- brokeshire". https://www.westerntelegraph.co.uk/pembrokeshirefarmer/10151047.half-of-all-welsh-big-cat-sightings-are-in-pembrokeshire/.

Wikipedia. "Little England beyond Wales". https://en.wikipedia.org/wiki/Little_England_beyond_Wales.

About the Author

George C. Hill, MA is a Pembrokeshire boy from the little coastal village of Penally. George spent his twenties in London gaining a History BA and failing miserably to break through with various musical outfits in the capital. His early thirties were a chequered affair working variously and disparately as a high-end restaurant manager, busker, educational recruitment consultant, and then moving from London to Budapest to become a songwriter for a Hungarian 'superband' Omega! Lately, George went back into education at London Metropolitan University, gaining a Distinction in an 'Organised Crime and Global Security' Master's. This largely research-based course with heavy emphasis on written interpretations of worldly historic cultural and political affairs rekindled George's interest in, and love of writing. The world and all its mystery in 2020/21 did deem it necessary to land Mr Hill back in the West, in the place he does indeed profess to love the best, with not much else to do but write. 'Its Way Out in the West!' was the outcome. George lives here and there, with no family of his own, no debt, no money and no doubt.

Printed in Great Britain
by Amazon